Thinking Together

THINKING TOGETHER

Making Meetings Work

V. A. Howard, Ph.D., and J. H. Barton, M.A.

William Morrow and Company, Inc.
New York

It is the policy of William Morrow and Company, Inc., and its imprints and affiliates, recognizing the importance of preserving what has been written, to print the books we publish on acid-free paper, and we exert our best efforts to that end.

Library of Congress Cataloging-in-Publication Data

Howard, V. A., 1937–
    Thinking together / V. A. Howard and J. H. Barton.
      p.   cm.
    ISBN 0-688-09747-2
    1. Discussion. 2. Forums (Discussion and debate)—Planning.
  3. Thought and thinking—Study and teaching. I. Barton, J. H.
  II. Title.
  LC6515.H65   1991
  371.3'7—dc20   91-13726
                                             CIP

Printed in the United States of America

First Edition

1 2 3 4 5 6 7 8 9 10

To Israel Scheffler
whose life and work exemplify
the union of logical thought
with humane thoughtfulness

Acknowledgments

This book is the product of many minds, as befits the topic of reasoning in groups. The authors are fortunate to have been associated not only with leading scholars but also with business people whose work it is to teach and to share the benefits of their experiences with others.

Our general understanding of how to design and conduct live inquiry owes much to Professor Israel Scheffler, Co-director, Philosophy of Education Research Center at Harvard; Dr. David N. Perkins, Co-director, Harvard Project Zero; Dr. J. Sterling Livingston, Chairman, Sterling Institute, Inc.; John W. Humphrey, Chairman and Chief Executive Officer, The Forum Corporation; Richard C. Whitely, Vice-Chairman of Forum; John J. Bray, Chief Executive, Forum Europe; Dr. T. G. Roupas, Manager, AEtna Institute for Corporate Education; and Drs. David MacMullen and Hans Picker, management consultants.

We are also in the debt of LeRoy Malouf, President, and William E. LeClere, Executive Vice President, LMA Associates; Paul Jarvie, Principal, Jarvie and Alexander; Dr. George H. Litwin, consultant; Scott Parry, President, Training House; Donald L. Somers, President, Universal Topics, Inc.; Robert Stringer, President, Sherbrooke Associates, Inc.; Stevan K. Trooboff, President and Chief Executive Officer, Carlson Travel Network; David McKeon, Second Vice President, Retirement Plans Marketing, The New England; and Gerald F. Walsh, consultant to the Gillette Company worldwide.

We would also like to acknowledge specific contributions to our thinking. From Israel Scheffler we learned what it is for a human being in professional surroundings to embody the values of honesty, objectivity, and respect. His thought pervades our book. From Stephen Seidel, doctoral candidate in the Harvard Graduate School of Education, we learned how actors cope with stage fright. His research on that topic influenced our treatment of discussion anxiety in Chapter Two. From J. Sterling Livingston we learned to look upon goal-setting and action-planning as part of a recursive process. Our treatment of those subjects in Chapters Five and Six reflects his thinking; also the thinking of Gerald Walsh, from whom we learned that one of the best ways of finding out where you want to go is to begin trying to get there; and also the thinking of John E. Miller, National Field Sales Manager for the Personal Care Division of Gillette, who taught us the importance of setting goals to deliver value to the customer. From Scott Parry, we learned much about the thinking of Robert F. Mager, whose works we draw on in our treatment of goal-setting and problem analysis in Chapters Five and Seven. From T. G. Roupas we learned the tough lesson of how to boil our ideas down to their essentials while laughing all the way. From our mutual friend and editorial consultant, John MacLean, we learned the importance of not assuming you know what someone means before they've hardly opened their mouths.

Special thanks go to Dr. Badi Foster, former President, AEtna Institute for Corporate Education, for providing a forum for the testing and elaboration of many of the ideas contained herein; to Maria Guarnaschelli, Senior Editor, William Morrow and Company, Inc., for her always sensible advice during the production stages; to Elvind Allan Boe, copy editor for William Morrow, for his editorial marksmanship; to Gerard F. McCauley, our literary agent, for his support and patience through all the delays; to Dr. Robert Payton, former Director, Exxon Education Foundation, who first urged us to explore the educational relevance of group inquiry; to the Exxon Education Foundation itself for past financial support; and to the Latsis Foundation for its financial support of the Philosophy of Education Research Center during the writing.

No doubt the book could be better. But for the generous help of the aforementioned, it would be much worse. All the errors and lapses are ours.

V.A.H.
J.H.B.
Cambridge, Massachusetts

Contents

Introduction and Overview

This book is intended for all of you who want to engage effectively in *rational discussion,* doing good thinking together with others and helping them do good thinking with each other, engaging in a process of *inquiry,* presenting and defending and challenging your own opinions and those of others through a *dialogue of discovery,* not to win debating points but rather to learn what you think and to gain wisdom and to act wisely.

Perhaps you're students or teachers, administrators or executives, managers or employees, consultants or researchers, buyers or sellers, citizens or public servants. Perhaps you want to identify opportunities, set priorities, make decisions and evaluate results. Perhaps you want to learn something, invent something or clarify something, or develop your understanding or find out where you stand. Whoever you are and whatever your aims, we're seeking to help you acquire the skills you need—both the *social* skills and the *intellectual* skills, including the skills to *plan* and *lead* discussion, the skills to *participate* in dialogue and the skills to *master* the *anxieties* that can cripple performance.

In good bookstores and libraries you'll find many titles on how to run meetings, how to negotiate, how to convince people and how to manage organizations—all tasks that require discussion with others. But you won't find a comprehensive treatment of rational discussion in any of those titles, nor will you find a book devoted to it. By contrast, we address both the intellectual and social requirements of inquiry, including the cognitive skills to plan and the cognitive and behavioral skills to lead and participate. We recommend approaches to stage fright based on research in cognitive therapy and the performing arts. We illustrate effective everyday reasoning and describe how you can initiate and sustain productive inquiry by choosing an appropriate leadership role. We present models for planning and conducting inquiry into subjects that frequently require serious rational discussion, including goals, plans, and problems. We also recommend approaches for taking notes as a means for leading discussion as well as creating a record of it.

In Chapter One, "On the Nature of Rational Discussion," we identify the values of inquiry and describe generally how you honor them in practice. We also contrast the dialogue of discovery with casual conversation, formal debate, and formal negotiation. We describe common forms of rational discussion and the general purposes for which it is usually conducted.

In Chapter Two, "Overcoming Stage Fright," we explore ways to address anxieties that may be keeping you from engaging in rational discussion with others effectively.

In Chapter Three, "Choosing a Leadership Role," we study the process of everyday reasoning, identify the leader's options for initiating and sustaining that process and describe six different approaches to the tasks of leadership.

In Chapter Four, "Preparing a Discussion Plan," we describe and illustrate plans of varying complexity, noting that detailed plans are frequently required when people meet to perform the key tasks explored in the chapters immediately following, that is, in Chapter Five, "Analyzing Situations and Setting Goals," and in Chapter Six, "Making and Evaluating Action Plans," and in Chapter Seven, "Identifying the Causes of Problems."

In Chapter Eight, "Announcing and Doing the Groundwork for a Discussion," we call attention to requirements for selecting and readying a site and preparing people to participate effectively in live inquiry. We also consider reasons why not to issue a call for rational discussion.

In Chapter Nine, "Behaving Thoughtfully: The Do's and Don'ts," we identify and discuss a wide variety of appropriate and inappropriate ways to initiate and advance the dialogue of discovery by asking questions, by listening and responding to others, by supporting and opposing others, and also by addressing key issues and strong differences of opinion.

In Chapter Ten, "On Taking Notes: From Thinking Aloud to Thinking on Paper," we explore the cognitive process and the practical mechanics of recording, organizing, and summarizing the results of live inquiry, inlcuding the mechanics of note-taking as a mode of leadership.

We invite you to read our book piecemeal, if you like, beginning with Chapter One, "On the Nature of Rational Discussion," if you're new to the subject or curious about it; or, if need be, beginning with Chapter Two, "Overcoming Stage Fright," remembering, however, that performance anxiety can cripple not just the novice but also the acclaimed master at the height of her or his career.

You might begin with Chapter Three, "Choosing a Leadership Role," and Chapter Four, "Preparing a Leadership Plan," and continue on through Chapters Five, Six, and Seven if you're primarily interested in how to plan for rational discussion generally or for rational discussion of particular key tasks.

You might begin with Chapter Eight, "Announcing and Doing the Groundwork for a Discussion," and continue on through Chapter Nine, "Behaving Thoughtfully: The Do's and Don'ts," and Chapter Ten, "On Taking Notes: From Thinking Aloud to Thinking on Paper," if you're primarily interested in the technical, political, and interpersonal aspects of conducting live inquiry, and also in the critical intellectual task of converting oral thinking into written thinking.

CHAPTER 1

On the Nature of Rational Discussion

Rational discussion is a cognitive enterprise, a dialogue of discovery, an innovative process of *inquiry* through which you seek greater knowledge and *critical understanding* of a subject by proposing, developing, and *evaluating* ideas about it. As we use the term here, we mean a collaborative process of thinking together with others rather than a process pursued privately on paper or within your own mind. We also mean a process you can put to such practical purposes as discovering what to do and how to do it.

To engage in rational discussion requires you honor the values of *respect* and *honesty* and *frankness* and *objectivity*. You demonstrate serious interest in the subject, you attend to differing and competing views, you listen carefully, and you show that you're willing to change your mind. You also try to see things as others do, to give all sides a hearing, to look beyond winning and losing, to set aside prejudice and preconception. You make

17

known to others the assumptions that govern your assertions. You urge others to make their assumptions
known. You encourage others to take account of all relevant evidence, arguments, and facts. You also resist any
rush to premature judgment.

Very importantly, you also contribute to inquiry not
simply by offering a case of your own but also by *questioning* the evidence, *contesting* the arguments, and
doubting the facts presented by others; in other words,
you contribute by offering *dissent.* That's what distin-
quishes rational discussion from all other forms of discourse: Respectfully, honestly, frankly, and objectively,
you dissent from the views of others, so that you and
they both may *learn* together.

The stated or implied purposes of rational discussion
vary with the setting. Public forums and televised panel
shows are intended for the education and entertainment
of a general audience, while academic and professional
seminars are intended for the education of specialists and
advancement of knowledge. The subject of discussion in
such educational settings is typically a question, issue, or
topic such as the following.

- "When Does Diplomacy Become an Extension of
  War by Other Means?

- "Fair Play in Sports: The Ideal. The Reality"

- "Evil as Defined in Melville Through the Drama of
  Battle Against It"

In educational settings, leaders of rational discussion
often face the challenge of getting people to *quiet down,*
for participants often have an unspoken private agenda—
to get themselves published loudly, early, and often.

In public or private enterprise, the setting for rational

discussion is often a formal staff meeting. People gather to talk for the stated or implied purposes of *informing themselves, making a decision,* or *preparing to make a decision.* The subject of discussion is typically a question, issue, or topic such as the following.

- "Should We Buy New Equipment or Lease It?"

- "Advertising to Fill Management Positions: What Works and What Doesn't."

- "Evaluating Productivity in the Human Resource Development Department."

Leaders of rational discussion in public and private enterprise often face the challenge of getting people to *speak up,* for participants often have the unspoken private agenda of protecting themselves against personal attack or protecting working relationships they see as too fragile to survive any discourse where people ask questions and express doubts. To honor the values of rational discussion under such conditions frequently requires the leader to practice the skills of the diplomat, conducting inquiry with people in private, carrying anonymous messages from one person to another, and carefully rehearsing the formal meeting where everyone will be on display, making it safe for people to say publicly and constructively what they previously had feared would be risky or destructive to say. Both authors have found themselves carrying such messages and allaying such fears in big organizations, recognizing that the values of inquiry may first have to be honored quietly in private before they can be honored fully in public.

Generally, when people say, "Let's discuss it," they mean, "Let's look into it together, seriously, keeping an open mind, because it's something important to do or to know about." Or else they mean, "Let's look into it because we might find out something new, different, important, surprising, or exciting." Generally, people do not mean, "Let's pass the time of day conversing about it pleasantly, *never* seriously, and changing the subject whenever we please."

Rational discussion is an open, focused, serious, collaborative *dialogue of discovery* where you *speak so that you can hear.* In stating you opinion, you *invite* others to *differ.* You *listen* to their differing views and offer differing views of your own; moreover, you don't merely *exchange views* with others; rather, you *change* your own views. You state your opinions *experimentally,* for the purpose of *testing* your thinking and *developing* your understanding. The dialogue of rational discussion is a form of "exploratory discourse" in which you *want* to hear *counterarguments.** If you're listening, the best counterarguments you hear may come from yourself.

Rational discussion requires listening of a kind you can't do when you're exhorting, haranguing, orating, or declaiming, or when you're catechizing people, looking for ready-made answers to ready-made questions. To participate in a dialogue of discovery, you have to prepare yourself to listen even as you speak, conscious that you don't know what you're going to hear in reply. In addition, you also must listen to others *all the way through to the end* of what they're saying, not interrupting them overtly with your speaking voice, declaring, "*I* know what you mean." Nor can you *interrupt people with your mental voice,* preparing and rehearsing your rejoinder because you've concluded from their class, age, gender, address, accent, appearance, religion, politics, occupation, education, sexual preference, material interest, or

*Kinneavy 1980, *passim* and especially pp. 186–88.

national or regional origin that you know what they mean before they've hardly started saying it. Nor can you interrupt people overtly or covertly by *attributing motives* to them, declaring, either to them or to yourself, "*I* know why you're saying that."

Rational discussion presupposes a sufficient commonalty of interest to permit cooperative and creative intellectual use of doubt and dissent. By comparison, a conversation doesn't suppose a commonalty of interest, a debate is an adversary proceeding, and negotiations presuppose a *lack* of commonalty of interest.

People generally converse for openly social purposes and sometimes for the covert purpose of gathering intelligence without directly asking for information. Purely social conversation is *respectful;* however, there's nothing necessarily *honest* about it, much less anything *frank* and *objective.* Conversation isn't a cognitive enterprise. It's a type of *courtship.*

Debates are characterized by *competitive argument,* not by open, collaborative rational dialogue. Formal debates are highly cognitive enterprises in which the argument is rational rather than tendentious. Typically, the subject is a deliberately provocative statement, for example, "Resolved: That Free Trade Is Inimical to Freedom." The debaters are assigned to present and defend positions for and against the resolution. Then they engage in an adversary proceeding, arguing *solely for* their position and *solely against* the opposing position. *Respect* counts, but *honesty, frankness,* and *objectivity* don't count at all, for the purpose is to win the argument rather than to use argument to inquire into truth. By contrast, no one can be said to "win" a rational discussion.

Negotiators often expend great effort to help contending parties honor the values of inquiry (Fisher and Ury, 1983; Fisher and Brown, 1989). But the fundamental purpose of negotiation is to make compromise possible and enable contending parties to come to terms, not to make rational discussion possible (Fisher and Ury, 1983). Contending parties can negotiate successfully without *learning* anything; in fact, they don't even have to talk to each other. They can reach agreement through agents or mediators.

For a discussion to be rational, the parties to it don't necessarily have to agree to anything. They can equally agree to agree, disagree, adjourn, or punt. What they do have to do is *work together* to *learn* something.

Rational discussion always involves learning; moreover, as a form of inquiry, it always retains its *educational* nature no matter what people use it for. Whatever the task, if people are honoring the values of inquiry, if they're making creative intellectual use of dissent, *and* if they're changing their minds or making up their minds because they're *learning* something from each other, then they're engaged in rational discussion.

Rational discussion makes possible a constructive market. Buyers and sellers use it to learn about each other, evaluate business conditions, align their objectives, decide what to do, and establish or continue productive relationships.

Rational discussion can be put to discrete practical purposes. For example, see Chapter Five of this book, "Analyzing Situations and Setting Goals," Chapter Six, "Making and Evaluating Action Plans," and Chapter Seven, "Identifying the Causes of Problems."

On television, rational discussion is staged and often is rehearsed and edited for the primary purpose of entertaining and enlightening the audience. The host or moderator or interviewer wants to attract and hold *your* attention, to educate and inform *you,* to get *you* thinking and help *you* think and keep *you* tuned. She engages the people on her show in inquiry primarily for *your* benefit,

not for *theirs*. Her job is not to help others think together and learn from each other, but rather to help *you*
think by proxy. Accordingly, we recommend you study
her with care if you're considering using her as model
of how to lead a rational discussion.

First make certain that you're studying her actual
practice and actual results. The questions you see and
hear her asking on her taped and edited show may not
be the questions she actually asked. What you see and
hear, she may have taped later. In addition, many of her
questions may have been edited out, along with many
uninteresting remarks by participants and incoherent exchanges between them.

Next make certain that what is appropriate practice
for her is appropriate practice for you. Because she's
staging inquiry for the benefit of an audience, she'll often
use force in ways we wouldn't recommend to any leader
of a seminar or staff meeting. For example, to maintain
sharp focus when time is at a premium, on news shows
and many panel shows, she frequently won't allow people to talk to each other except as she directs. In addition, to avoid dead air that could cause viewers to change
channels, she'll often break in when no one is talking,
cutting short what might have been a period of productive silent thinking in other settings. Also, to prevent
viewers from becoming confused, she'll politely but
quickly interrupt a digression that in other settings might
have led to development of significant ideas.

To determine what's appropriate practice for you, we
recommend that you read Chapter Three of this book,
"Choosing a Leadership Role," Chapter Four, "Preparing a Discussion Plan," and Chapter Nine, "Behaving
Thoughtfully: The Do's and Don'ts." In Appendix A,
"Suggested Viewing," we list regularly scheduled television programs for critical, comparative study.

CHAPTER 2

Overcoming Stage Fright

STAGE FRIGHT: EMOTIONAL SOURCES

Perhaps you are a new employee, MBA freshly in hand, attending your first sales meeting in the marketing division of Electronics International. Perhaps you are an undergraduate enrolled in your first course in logic. Or perhaps you are a government official attending an important committee meeting. Your palms are sweating; your heart is beating wildly; your breathing is shallow; your throat is dry; you can't seem to focus on what is being said; everyone else seems so confident, so smart, so at ease; you feel so stupid, so out of place, so afraid. "God, please don't let them ask me anything; let me disappear!" And suddenly, the inevitable happens. Someone, the sales manager, the instructor, a colleague, turns to you and says, "Well, Joan, what's your opinion on that?"

Flight or fight. It's a natural human response to perceived danger. Something in you decides to flee. "Well, I just don't know; I mean, I dunno . . . um." The oth-

24

ers look away and carry on without you. You feel miserable. Or something in you decides to fight. "Ha! You really had to put me on the spot, didn't you? Well, my opinion is that this is all nonsense and a waste of time." Again, the others look away and carry on without you. You feel miserable. Overreact either way, you lose.

Take a less threatening situation. The discussion is quite casually conducted. There is no pressure on anyone to speak up. Some do, some don't. You are one of those who don't. You sit there, listening, keeping quiet, laying back, letting it all happen without participating, observing the principle of least effort—in effect, underreacting. At least you aren't embarrassed or exposed. But you are paying a price for your passivity: your opinions are not heard; your queries go unanswered; you have no voice in the matter under discussion. Nothing *you* think makes the least difference. Though you feel safe, you still feel miserable.

Whether you overreact or underreact in any of these ways, your emotions have gotten the better of you, preventing you from participating effectively in the discussion. Is there anything you can do about it? There is, and the first thing is to take note of the following two propositions:

1. Emotions are seldom "free-floating": they don't just happen; they are caused by your *interpretation* of events. For example, you don't, as a rule, feel fear unless you *think* a particular person, thing, or event is a threat to you.

2. Whatever you think about the topic under discussion, how you feel about the *situation* you are in is at least in part caused by how you think about (and to) yourself *in that situation*. To put it simply, most strong emotions originate in particular thoughts, whether those

thoughts are true or false, realistic or outlandish (Burns 1980, pages 38–39).

STAGE FRIGHT: COGNITIVE SOURCES

Fear of speaking up to others often has its origins in how we talk to ourselves; that is, the fleeting, silent thoughts triggered off by stressful situations. Perhaps you are saying to yourself, "Better to feel miserable than to risk looking foolish, making a mistake, showing my ignorance, or offending anyone. . . . I don't understand a thing, better shut up. . . . If I open my mouth these people will jump all over me. . . . What's bothering me just isn't worth bothering about. . . . My opinions count for nothing in this company." Or perhaps a series of more aggressive, hostile thoughts flashes through your mind. "What the hell do these people know? . . . I just don't like this; I don't want to be here. . . . These people are deliberately talking over my head, ignoring me. . . . Talk is cheap." And so on and on in self-destructive commentary. Swimming in and out of consciousness with the speed of barracudas, these "inner voices" can torment and paralyze you into silence as effectively as if a hand were clapped over your mouth.

Of course, your inner voices could be right in any given situation. Depending upon the circumstances, you may be well-advised to keep quiet or to dismiss the whole proceeding. If you are rudely put on the spot or ignored by a hostile instructor, manager, or colleague, a defensive reaction is normal. But if one or other of the patterns of overreaction or underreaction described above is your *usual* response to discussion situations, particularly formal discussions such as business meetings or classes, then you are suffering from stage fright.

You are not alone. Stage fright is not confined to actors and musicians. It afflicts teachers, students, business people, politicians—indeed, anyone who is called upon to "perform" in public. Discussion stage-fright refers to whatever *inner,* personal obstacles prevent you from participating effectively in a discussion.

STAGE FRIGHT: COMMONSENSE SOURCES

Aside from the aforementioned patterns of under-reaction and overreaction, mostly rooted in fear or hostility, discussion stage-fright has two further "commonsense" sources. First is the expectation that you must get all your ideas straight and clear *before* you speak; that somehow disaster will ensue if you fail to articulate your views or opinions perfectly the first time. Second is the assumption that thinking necessarily precedes talking, that speech is but a verbalized encapsulation of previously worked-out ideas. Both notions not only inhibit your ability to participate in a discussion but are also fatal to the very idea of discussion itself.

Now admittedly, there are many times when "think before you speak" is good advice. But in a genuine discussion, in an atmosphere of exploratory discourse, the whole point of talking is to expand your understanding of a topic or issue, not to utter perfectly worded preconceived opinions. Putting exact statement and fully formed opinion before the spirit of inquiry reverses the priorities of discussion. You engage in discussion precisely in order to find that better formulation, question, or solution. It is as if you were to say, "I will not search for the solution to my problem until I have it," a stultifying stance, to say the least.

The assumption that thinking necessarily precedes talking denies the obvious fact that talking is a way of thinking, an instrument of thought, as much as writing can be (Howard and Barton 1986, pages 20–22). You think *by* talking, particularly in a dialogue where the give-and-take of question and answer is the very process of thinking itself. The wonderful thing about language as a symbolic system is that it allows us to think to ourselves silently, to think on paper in writing, or to think aloud to others in speech. Reducing all thinking to silent, inner speech simply ignores the other manifestations of thinking in writing and discussion. In other words, you may think before you speak or write or *as* you speak or write. Discussion is a case of *thinking as you and others speak to each other.*

THERAPY FOR STAGE FRIGHT

Severe cases of stage fright may require psychiatric or medical treatment (Lockwood 1989); but for most people, a little self-help "therapy" will suffice to reduce if not eliminate most of the psychological obstacles to participating in a discussion, especially those pesky, self-destructive inner voices. Having once lowered the emotional and psychological barriers to participating in a discussion, you will also need to master certain *logical and social* strategies; but these will be taken up in later chapters. Right now, let's concentrate on lowering your anxiety about speaking up in public.

We suggest two strategies for confronting your inner voices, one we called the Method of Objectification, the other the Method of Personification. The appeal of the former is that it is logical, literal, and objective; the appeal of the latter is that it is psychological, metaphoric, and personal. Both are rational. Depending upon your temperament, and whether you prefer to put problems at a psychological distance or keep them close to you,

you may want to choose one or the other or a combination of both.

The Method of Objectification

The Method of Objectification is derived from recent developments in cognitive therapy.* The basic strategy is very simple but requires some diligence in application. It consists of three steps, all of which, to be most effective, should be done *in writing.* That means keeping a notepad at hand during those moments of greatest anxiety. This sounds like asking a lot, but, for once, it is something easier done than said. The steps are as follows:

Step 1: Record in writing as best you can exactly what your inner voices say to you at the moments of greatest stress.

Step 2: Identify in writing the errors of reasoning involved in what the inner voices say to you.

Step 3: Reply in writing to those voices in the most balanced, reasonable way you can.

While you are on the spot, Steps 2 and 3 may have to be deferred to a later time; but Step 1 is essential to the whole strategy, and it must be carried out with ruthless honesty. Don't edit your thoughts. Just record them as quickly and as literally as you can. For example, if

---

*Cognitive therapy is a method of treating depression. It was pioneered by Dr. Aaron T. Beck (1972) and was further explored more recently by Dr. David D. Burns in his *Feeling Good: The New Mood Therapy* (1980). Though stage fright differs from depression, many of the same strategies for combating the latter apply to the former. Herein, we present an adaptation of cognitive therapy solely for purposes of diminishing the illogical and emotional causes of the former.

your first thoughts upon sitting down are, "Oh hell, what am I doing here? I don't know the first thing about what's going on," *write that down.*

From then on, whenever you can steal a second or two, scribble down whatever the inner voices are telling you. Don't focus on how you feel. It's clear that you feel humiliated, frightened, insecure. Focus instead on what the voices are telling you that causes those feelings: in other words, not, "I feel so threatened," but "I'll never be able to answer properly if they ask me anything" (cf. Burns 1980, page 68). You may be able to recall additional items later on, but your thoughts at the moments of stress will be the most vivid and honest. And remember that honesty with yourself at those moments is not only the best policy; it's the best way of collecting "data" for later analysis. And that analysis will, in turn, help get you out of the fix you are in.

Step 1 is essentially a recording activity, one that only you can perform. Only you can know what ideas are flitting through your mind in the circumstances in which you find yourself. You will get better at "fishing for the barracudas" the more you try. Many will of course escape your hook, but the ones you catch will likely be the fiercest.

Let us now turn to the analytical stages of the Method of Objectification, in which you will learn how to confront and then to correct the inner voices.

ANALYZING THE INNER VOICES

The inner voices have spoken. The barracudas have struck. You've hooked a few. Now let's dissect them. The objective is to identify the logical errors, the distortions, the exaggerations, the gross generalizations, and plain falsehoods that lace the rhetoric of defeatism within.

Anxiety does not speak with a forked tongue; it speaks with a thoroughly negative tongue, and that is its weakness *when exposed*. Your job now is to expose those weaknesses. This is Step 2, and here's how to do it.

First, learn to recognize "cognitive distortions," the ways in which the inner voices chronically delude us, distort reality and aggravate anxiety (Burns 1980, pages 41–50). Following are five types of cognitive distortion, ways we aggravate the anxiety of speaking up in a discussion.

1. *All-or-Nothing Dogmatism.* All-or-nothing dogmatism is thinking in terms of absolutes: absolute dichotomies ("If I have nothing to say, I'm a failure"); absolute labels ("I'm just dumb, an idiot"); absolute perfection ("I have to be brilliant; everyone expects it"); absolute demands ("My brief was the best one, and they'd better accept it"); and absolute judgments ("I'm right, they're wrong, and no compromise"). Indeed, all-or-nothing thinking is essentially an attitude of "no compromise," ever, on anything. Things are this way or that and no other way, black or white, no shades of gray, no alternatives but those you see.

Extremist dogmatic thinking has at least three debilitating effects: it closes your mind (so no need to discuss the matter); it blinds you to the subtleties of reality (so no need to inquire further); and it cuts you off from your colleagues (so no need to talk to them). And in its perfectionist mode it makes all progress impossible, for nothing you or anyone else does will ever be good enough.

2. *Hasty Generalization.* Hasty generalization is the tendency to make blanket statements of universal scope on the basis of limited evidence or samples. "Managers *never* understand the problems of the sales staff." *"No-*

body pays any attention to me." "I *always* have to learn the hard way." "*All* academics are stuffy eggheads." "We can't *ever* settle this issue." "*Nothing* good ever happens to me." "I'm *totally* unable to learn this stuff." "This idea of mine is *completely* worthless." "I wasn't promoted this round, so it's *impossible* for me to get ahead in this company." One case, one instance of defeat, disappointment, or failure is usually enough to send the powers of hasty generalization running rampant. "Surely, because I misunderstood the manager's point, I am dumb now, always was, and always shall be."

Sometimes it is enough merely to drag a hasty generalization, or any of these distortions of thought, into the open to see how absurd it is. But when they flash through your mind, unchallenged, freely associating with your other, saner, thoughts, they can wreak havoc on your confidence. Hasty generalization also is the mechanism by which we transform any momentary unpleasantness into permanent unpleasantness. "Just my luck—always!" you say, when you find a dent in the fender of your car, despite the fact that you've been driving the car for two years without incident. The dent is bad enough, but singling yourself out as destined for dents by a malign Lady Luck only makes matters worse.

3. *Accentuating the Negative.* To accentuate the negative is to ignore the positive aspects of a situation, focus solely on the negative aspects, and exaggerate their importance. The cup is never half-full; it's always half-empty. You distort reality by constantly whispering to yourself, "If you can't say something negative, don't say anything at all."

For example, you are giving a formal sales presentation and a page is missing from your report. You send someone to retrieve it from the photocopier and go on.

But for the rest of the day you can think of nothing but that minor gaffe until, by day's end, it is magnified into a major gaffe and the beginning of the end of your career. "Oh, God, I was so embarrassed. So stupid! How could I forget that page? They even laughed. My credibility is completely blown. Nobody who is any good would make that mistake. I'm really not cut out for this kind of work." What began as a trivial interruption ends by being (in your mind only) a catastrophe. Such exaggeration of negative details fills you with apprehension and gloom, blinding you to the real worth of your work.

Again, assume that this was your first formal presentation to a highly competent group. While a bit unsteady, perhaps, you manage to get your points across and receive warm thanks. Now, rather than seeing yourself as gradually coming up to speed in fast professional company, you dwell instead on the shortfall between your performance and that of others. "I wasn't clear enough. I didn't respond to questions as well as Fred. I wasn't as poised in my delivery as Alice. My flip charts weren't as well done as George's." And so on and on until the mountain of your accomplishments up to now is reduced to a molehill of mediocrity. And what about those warm thanks at the end of your presentation? "Oh well, they had to say that. They were just being polite." At this point nothing positive remains. "What's wrong with me? Can't I do anything right?" Question begging now joins forces with the power of negative thinking just to make sure you don't get away with anything good.

Accentuating negative details, filtering them out and obsessing about them, is debilitating enough; but when such details are exaggerated in importance, blown out of proportion, reality is the first casualty. (Your self-esteem is the second.) A balanced self-assessment of your performance is automatically ruled out. As well, you are left in a state of narrow vision and diminished confidence with virtually no hope of improvement, since you stubbornly refuse to acknowledge anything positive in what you did.

4. *Expecting the Worst.* Expecting the worst results in presumptions about what negative things *must* be going on in other people's minds and about what unpleasantness the future *must* hold for you and for you alone. Because someone at the conference table seems preoccupied, you think, "They're not listening, they think I'm boring. They're passing judgment on me right now." Later, when you receive warm thanks for your effort, you think, "They're hiding what they really think about me. They just want to get me out of the way as quickly as possible. They don't give a damn about what I said." So you withdraw into surly silence or respond rudely to "phony" compliments and thanks. What you hastily presume to be going on in other people's minds causes you to respond inappropriately or awkwardly to what they actually say and do. That behavior in turn can eventually cause them to think about you exactly as you now (falsely) presume!

Negative mind-reading is especially dangerous when combined with negative expectations about the future. For instance, before the conference, you may say to yourself, "I just know that I'm going to blow this presentation. I'm so nervous that I'll never calm down. I'll forget everything I have to say. They don't respect me anyway. One question and I'll fall apart. I know it, I know it." Then, of course, at the first sign of any conceivable threat (just walking into the conference room may do it) or possible criticism (that yawn was aimed directly at you, certainly; that smile was obviously insincere), you may well begin to fall apart. Not, however, because of anything you *knew,* but because of everything you *presumed*. Your negative mind-reading and fortune-telling have become negative *self-fulfilling prophecies,* bringing about the very circumstances you most fear.

After all, the apparent preoccupation of just one person in the room says nothing about the others. Besides, there are a hundred reasons why that person may be preoccupied that have nothing to do with you. And the person who yawned may only be tired from a sleepless night. And the thanks and compliments most likely are sincere. But your exclusively negative hypotheses about what other people are thinking and what the future holds for you allow for none of that.

5. *Name-calling.* Name-calling produces the negative and exaggerated labels we hang round our necks like albatrosses whenever something goes wrong. "Oh, hell, I left that page in the photocopier. What an *idiot* I am! What a *fool*! How could I be so *stupid?*" Worse yet, as a side effect of negative mind-reading and fortune-telling, you may unjustly hang those labels round the necks of others. "These *pompous asses* are utterly obtuse. Such *hypocrites*! *Blind mice!*"

Name-calling and other negative labeling is a form of prejudice—witness the hateful power of such words as *nigger, wop, spic, honky,* and the like. Less commonly acknowledged is how we torture ourselves with prejudicial labels. One fumbling response and you are a "born loser." A little confusion about a particular point and you are a "cretin." Somebody yawns while you are speaking and you are a "dullard." Worse yet, somebody asks you a question you are not prepared for and that person becomes a "trickster."

Insecurity breeds *prejudice,* not only *against others* but *against oneself,* and the destructive effects are the same: alienation, hostility, insensitivity, and unfairness. It's bad enough to be unfair to others, but perhaps the ultimate injustice is unfairness to oneself—the root of all injustice. Name-calling is not only self-demeaning, it is a form of bigotry aimed at yourself.

Our brief descriptions and examples of cognitive distortion hardly exhaust the rhetoric of defeatism, but they do give you a basis for understanding how the destructive rhetoric of your inner voices works. Now you can take Step 2 of cognitive therapy for discussion stagefright by identifying in writing the errors of reasoning committed by your inner voices.

First search your memory for examples of the five types of cognitive distortion:

- All-or-Nothing Dogmatism
- Hasty Generalization
- Accentuating the Negative
- Expecting the Worst
- Name-calling

Try to recall at least one example of each type of distortion. Here's an example that includes more than one type: "If I cannot speak up right at this moment, then I'm a failure and a coward." That's an instance both of All-or-Nothing Dogmatism and Name-calling. Here's an example of three types of distortion: "I'll never understand this stuff. They don't really think I can. They're just being polite. I mean, I muffed two out of the five case studies." The first sentence is a Hasty Generalization, the second represents negative mind-reading, a form of Expecting the Worst, and the third and fourth sentences are examples of Accentuating the Negative, that is, ignoring the positive and exaggerating the importance of the negative. Your analyses don't have to be any more detailed than that; and don't worry about where your examples exactly fit, so long as you can identify at least *some* of the errors in what your inner voices say. You are now ready to go on to Step 3, where you talk back to your inner voices in writing.

TALKING BACK TO YOUR INNER VOICES

The method of talking back to your inner voices is one cognitive therapists call the "triple-column technique" (Burns 1980, page 67). It is both simple and explicit. The exercise of writing everything down takes the whole business out of the realm of free association and impression, placing matters on a plane of objectivity. You can see what you think, you can see what is wrong with it, and you can see your rational response. Importantly, for your responses to be effective, they must be rational—not wishful rationalizations—in other words, you must *believe* what you say in reply (Burns 1980, page 68).

Divide a page vertically into three columns. Label the first column "Inner Voices"; label the second column "Errors"; label the third column "Replies." Using the example from the end of the preceding section, Steps 1, 2, and 3 will look something like this:

Inner Voices	Errors	Replies
1. I'll never understand this stuff.	1. Hasty Generalization	1. Never? I already understand enough to ask questions. Besides, even if I don't master the material completely, I can surely grasp enough of it to do the job.

Inner Voices	Errors	Replies
2. They don't really think I can.	2. Expecting the Worst: negative mind-reading	2. Why would they waste their time instructing me if they really thought I could not learn this material? It doesn't make sense. It's just as likely that what they "really" think is that I *can* learn it.
3. They're just being polite.	3. Accentuating the Negative: ignoring the positive	3. Why shouldn't they be polite? They're polite to everybody, not just me. And nobody would take all this time, at great expense and effort, just to be polite.
4. I mean, I muffed two out of the five case studies.	4. Accentuating the Negative: exaggerating its importance	4. But I also solved three case studies. And the two I failed to get are clear to me now, so what's the big deal about missing two? Also, solving three cases shows that I *can* understand the material contrary to my inner voice number 1 above.

The common characteristic of all four replies is that they are rational, objective, there to be seen when the voices speak again, and realistic. They neither raise false hopes nor exaggerate your abilities; but they *do* truthfully assess the real situation and squash the influence of negative self-deception. The effects of the triple column technique are cumulative: the more you use it, the better at it you become; the better at it you become, the more effective it will be in combating the cognitive/emotional causes of discussion stage-fright. Talking back to your inner voices is a habit of *intra*personal dialogue that can free you to engage in *inter*personal dialogue.

The Method of Personification*

An even more direct, if less methodical, way of talking back to your inner voices is to cast them as "characters" in your own private psychodrama. No doubt, there will be plenty of candidates past and present: parents, teachers, friends, colleagues, spouses, your earlier selves—in childhood, adolescence, adulthood. Warning voices, worrying voices, critical voices, fearful voices, protecting voices—you carry them with you continuously, but they make their most vivid "appearances" at threatening moments. They stride onto your inner stage just when you are expected to perform, whispering their messages of fear, inadequacy, and escape.

They say routine, highly predictable things: "Be careful, you're in over your head." "This is too much for

*Partly suggested by Eloise Ristad's *A Soprano on Her Head* (1982), especially her Chapter 2, entitled "The Book of Judges." We are also indebted to Steven Seidel, doctoral candidate in the Harvard Graduate School of Education, whose research on stage fright and whose systematic elaborations on controlling performance anxiety greatly informed this section.

you." "You don't have what it takes for this." "Why are you letting yourself in for this?" "Who do you think you are?" "You don't belong in this company." "Please don't make a fool of yourself." "You always have to learn the hard way." Shadowy figures of a lifetime, they stalk the fringes of your mental stage, making it difficult for you to "go on." They won't go away. What can you do?

Don't deny them. Denial is a costly and futile effort. Instead, invite your *personae* in for a "conversation." Use your imagination to personify the inner voices and draw them out. See them in human form standing, sitting there before you exactly as they have evolved in your mental life. Very importantly, don't assume that they are entirely negative. Begin by assuming that they are friendly, so that they will *stop* and *listen* to you. After all, you are dealing with "persons" now, "characters," some of whom care about you and want to protect you from harm. They may be overly protective, defensive, critical, fearful, but they have your interests at heart.*

Be frank. Say, "I need to do this now, and you are saying not to. What are you worried about? I can hear your warning and still go on, and take my chances, can't I?" Negotiate with the voices. Ask, "What do you think will happen to me if I fail? Do you really want me to go through the next three months without saying a word? Why do you think I will fail? When *can* I speak up? Only when I am perfectly prepared? But that's unrealistic. You know that. So now what?" In effect, call the question. Put that character on the spot. Listen carefully to the "actor's" lines and the emotional tone of them. The idea is to put the fear in the *character*, in the voice. Then you become a bit braver. The fear is yours, but

---

*If, on the other hand, your characters do appear entirely negative, see Appendix B: "The Parliamentary Method."

you've displaced it onto the character who has stepped onto your stage.

Now you can begin to assert yourself, saying, to that character, "I'm going to go to the meeting reasonably well prepared. I'm going to listen for twenty minutes and decide for myself how many people are any better prepared. If I see that I've prepared well enough to make a contribution, I'm going to make one. I'll give you a chance to make your case. But, you have to go away when I decide to take my turn. You can come back later, but not before. You cannot come in and stop me, because this is something I really want to do and must do."

The trick here is to *dismiss* the character for the duration of your performance. That character has had his or her say; now it is your turn. There are a number of ways of signaling this dismissal: "When I leave this room, then you must leave me," or "When I put on this suit, . . ." or "When I walk on stage, . . ." or "When the boss asks me a question, . . ." or "When I have a real concern to air, . . ." The characters in your personal drama having been consulted and negotiated with, they must now be "sent away," to the anteroom, to the alley outside, to the wings of the stage, to the places of their origin, to the past. Let the wisdom reside in yourself, not in them—in your judgment, in your responses.

Such personification allows you to employ the discussion skills you already possess and move on from the inner dialogue to the outer dialogue. Each situation is taken as a separate struggle rather than a decisive battle. Neither you nor the characters in your inner drama will change overnight. Part of talking to them is giving up the *effort* of denying them. You accept their concerns, their fears, but you try to see this as a long-term situation that has to change. Again, be frank and practical with them. What have you to lose by speaking up? A bad report? Embarrassment? A loss of influence, of opportunity? Ask these characters what realistic risks are involved so you can make a balanced choice as to where or when not to speak up. If the only choice is to jump into the fire, that is *never* a good thing to do. But is that the situation here and now? If not, then get thee behind me!

Sensing danger, the characters in your inner drama will make their entrances on the brink of your performance. So prepare for them. One aspect of preparation is deciding, *Who* am I in this situation? What is my role? That follows from, What do I *want*? Create a character out of yourself. See yourself as what you want to be, the role you want to play, as having the frame of mind you want to have.

On the day of your real-life performance, choose a time to begin the inner dialogue with your characters. You cannot rehearse the specific lines except as a set speech, but you can assume a role for yourself: the employee with a reasonable question, the critic with a legitimate complaint, the student wanting to understand, the discussion leader soliciting opinions, the division head with an agenda to be covered. Then, when your inner characters challenge your "act," ask them, "How would you suggest I play this? If you have no useful suggestions, please step outside until I am finished."

The Method of Personification helps you focus on what you want to do and say, what you have to contribute, what matters to you. Once you have dealt with the concerns of your doubting Thomases and firmly but politely requested them to exit, you are freer to get on with your real-life performance. If you know your "part," your role in the situation, if you know who you are and what you want in that situation, you are ready to cope with the challenges it presents.

The Method of Personification for reducing stage fright is rather like *commedia dell'arte,* an improvisational form of theater involving conventional plots and roles and predictable characters, but *not* fixed dialogue. Each character plays a stock part in a few standard scenarios. If you know your part, your role, what you care about, and know what to expect from your doubting Thomases, you can deal with the challenges of the drama within and without. "Rehearsal" for the real play (e.g., the staff meeting, the class, the seminar) begins offstage in the preliminary encounter with characters you definitely do *not* want to take with you onstage. In his *Screwtape Letters,* C. S. Lewis (1962) observes that the devil would ideally like us to believe that he (the devil) doesn't exist, for then he is free to wreak his havoc. You know better. Your "devils" do exist, in your own mind. By confronting them dramatically, you avoid the dangers of denial while enhancing your own position of strength and control.

CHAPTER 3

Choosing a Leadership Role

TAKING CHARGE

Having overcome some of your personal blocks to participating in meetings, classes, seminars, you are now able to follow the lead of others by responding constructively to the questions that you and they have been asked to address. Then, one day, the section head, the professor, the CEO turns to you and says, "Olivia, I'd like you to run next week's discussion. I've watched you come out of your shell in recent weeks, so I know you can do it. By the way, it's a tough assignment." You feel triumph mixed with panic. Now *you* have to lead, make sure that people think things through and speak up constructively. What do you do? How do you make use of your experience up to now? The first thing is to remind yourself that *a discussion leader's primary responsibility is to guide discussion by asking questions, by anticipating replies, and by listening and responding to others.*

Your job as leader is to help people to talk reasonably to each other—as rational beings, and also as emotional and political beings: you want them to learn from each other, to reason together, to share their knowledge and experience. You want them to develop, express, and modify their opinions, and to challenge the opinions of others. And you want them to work well together, acknowledging their differences as legitimate and their feelings as respected.

Fine. So now what to do? Knowing your basic responsibility as leader, there are three more action steps to assuming leadership: first, acquaint yourself with the patterns of everyday reasoning for inquiry and problem solving; second, decide how much and what kinds of direction you want to give as leader; and third, choose a leadership role. We will now take you through each of these steps.

Reasoning for Inquiry and Problem Solving

Whatever the topic or task of the discussion you have been asked to lead, your first job is to manage that process of effective everyday reasoning we call *inquiry*. How do you inquire into and reason about a problem, an unanswered question, a troublesome situation? Mostly, you go about it in question-and-answer fashion in roughly four phases:

1. You assert or query what you *think* about an issue, including what it *means* to you—what you *know* about it, what you *believe* or *suspect* about it, how you *feel* about it.

2. You *challenge* your own thinking, questioning your version of the matter, your information, your beliefs, your attitudes.

3. You challenge *other people's versions,* including their assertions, beliefs, explanations, attitudes, and even what you imagine or infer them to think.

4. You respond to your own and others' opinions in a *continuing series of questions and replies.*

Whether you do this silently to yourself, aloud in discussion, or in writing, and whether you go through all four phases, reasoning itself tends to proceed in this way: from "hunches and first thoughts" to "reservations and misgivings" to "questions and challenges to others" to "replies to the objections." Often these phases will overlap or be repeated (Howard and Barton 1986, pages 66–70). Throughout the four phases, the operative questions are *What?*, *Why?*, and (from Phase 2 on) *Why not?* Asking them over and over of yourself and of others is the major stimulus to inventive reasoning.

What does such inquiry look like in an actual case? Research led by David N. Perkins of the Harvard Graduate School of Education shows that effective everyday reasoning proceeds by *challenging, changing,* and *abandoning* your opinions and assumptions while thinking through a problem. Starting with your first thoughts, you argue against them, thus generating second thoughts. Having further misgivings about your second thoughts, you come up with third thoughts on the issue, and so on in a series of replies and counterreplies. For example, suppose you've been asked whether a law requiring a five-cent deposit on bottles and cans would reduce litter. Here's how you might respond:

> The law wants people to return the bottles for five cents, instead of littering them. But I don't think five cents is enough nowadays to get people to bother.
>
> *But wait,* it isn't just five cents at a blow, because people can accumulate cases of bottles or bags of

cans in their basements and take them back all at once, so probably they would do that.

Still, those probably aren't the bottles and cans that get littered anyway; it's the people out on picnics or kids hanging around the streets and parks that litter bottles and cans, and they sure wouldn't bother to return them for a nickel.

But, someone else might—boy scout and girl scout troops and other community organizations very likely would collect the bottles and cans as a combined community service and fund-raising venture; I know they do that sort of thing. (Perkins et al. 1983, page 178; emphasis added)

Ignore for now whether you agree or disagree with the conclusion reached (after all, the thinking may go on). Attend instead to *how* it was reached. To paraphrase Perkins, you interrogate your knowledge base to construct arguments pro and con (page 186). You state an opinion, then challenge and change it through a series of premises as the reflective process goes on, thereby "elaborating your understanding of the situation" (page 178). In effect, you *discover* what you think. You use reasoning inventively to *create new knowledge and understanding,* not merely to test the validity, probability, or truth of conclusions already reached from premises already given. Of course, you may use reason for these and other purposes, but reasoning in discussion, in the service of live inquiry, reaches beyond anything given *to explore and make known what is unknown.* Otherwise, why bother to discuss anything?

What?, Why?, and *Why not?* lie at the core of everyday reasoning. They take different forms: *What exactly is the issue here? What am I trying to say? What is their position? Why is this idea, this proposal, this explanation a good one?* And conversely, *Why is this idea a bad one? Why would this plan fail?* To competent thinkers in every domain of thought, such questions become second nature, driving first thoughts on through objections and challenges to a conclusion. They propel us out of complacency and on to solving problems and devising better plans of action. Repeated over and over again, in hundreds of situations, they enable us to come up with the best ideas possible, which means the most plausible ideas imaginable.

Giving Guidance and More

Next you have to decide how much and what kinds of direction you want to give as leader. Basically, you have one obligation and three options:

- guide the discussion (obligation)

- control the discussion (option)

- join the discussion (option)

- help others to draw conclusions (option)

GUIDING THE DISCUSSION

This is the minimum you can do. You do it by asking questions, listening and responding to others, and often by summarizing what has been said. Guiding means *intervening impartially to maintain focus.* For example, "George, you had an issue you wanted to raise. Do you want to bring it up now or would later be better? Ann, you know about analyzing data. Could you tell us what you think data shows? Fred, you supervise the clinicians. Would you comment on Ann's findings?" This is the sort of timely intervention that keeps a discussion going and on track.

CONTROLLING THE DISCUSSION

Controlling a discussion does not mean telling people what to think. Rather, it means selecting topics, scheduling time limits, and urging people to use their time and energy effectively when they have a lot to talk about or when a decision has to be made, such as at board meetings, sales meetings, faculty senates, and professional conferences. In such settings, you can help people greatly by intervening directly. For example, "To start, I'd like to invite comments on our agenda. Should we add or delete anything? Restate something?" Or, "Could we come back to that point later on?" Or, "Would anyone like to add anything before we move on? We have three more items to deal with in the next hour."

However effective in some settings, strictly controlling direction can disrupt an open-ended discussion. For example, one of the authors recently served on a panel discussing the relationships between art and science. On the panel were a philosopher, an astronomer, a physicist, a composer, and a graphic artist. The panel was chaired by a graduate student in education, earnest but rather unsure of his ground. He had a list of questions to put to the panel, such as "What are your criteria for deciding when something is right or wrong, correct or incorrect in physics, in poetry, in musical composition?" and, "What is the nature of the discipline in your field?"

In response to both questions, the physicist began rather arrogantly, saying, "In physics we have strict criteria for experimental verification and the testing of hypotheses, but in art, I mean, if it feels good, do it!" "Hold on," replied the composer. "Are you saying that as artists we are playing tennis without a net? Have you ever been in a composer's studio or musician's practice room and witnessed what goes on there?" The philosopher chimed in, too: "The suggestion seems to be that art is without either discipline or standards of criticism. I find that distinctly odd." At about this point, the moderator interrupted what looked to become an amusing free-for-all (members of the audience were already thrusting their hands in the air) to announce that a lot of questions remained and the next one was . . . We on the panel all looked at each other in dismay while the audience squirmed in discomfort.

Obviously, the moderator tried to control too closely where he should have guided. He tried to get the panel to address a prepared list of questions, apparently thinking he was running a tightly scheduled group interview rather than an open-ended discussion. He might have intervened more propitiously by asking, "Could each of you, then, briefly describe or illustrate how critical standards work in your field?" By making that request, he would have forestalled a confrontation and given the discussion focus, setting it on a course of inquiry. Instead, he preemptively changed the subject just as it was getting interesting.

When you control a discussion, people expect you to influence the *course* of their thinking by setting an agenda, scheduling time, and calling for results. They also expect you to influence the *quality* of their thinking by urging them to address all relevant issues; however, they don't expect you or want you to influence the *content* of their thinking by joining the discussion, abandoning impartiality for advocacy.

JOINING THE DISCUSSION

When you're teaching a class or leading a seminar, directing a staff meeting, evaluating research results, or conducting a planning session, you may be expected to join in the discussion. That means contributing to the group's thinking substantively by offering your opinions and answering questions as well as asking them. Where you have relevant knowledge or experience, others may feel that you have an obligation to share it with them. If so, you cannot remain aloof from the proceedings as an *impartial* moderator; but you can show yourself to be a *fair-minded, even-handed* participant who advocates for the common good.

Joining a discussion is always a delicate decision. As a general rule, the more formal the discussion, the greater the risks of joining it. That is because you sacrifice the impartiality of a moderator for the partisan views of a participant. For a teacher, seminar leader, or research director, participation is expected and carries few procedural risks, provided you know what you are talking about. For a mentor in business or personnel training, not to participate would be equally out of place. But for a dean or moderator of a political discussion, to suddenly leap in with urgency could be fatal—tantamount to abdication of the role of dean, or moderator. In proportion to your mandate to control (not merely to guide) a discussion, you are prevented from actively participating in it.

HELPING PARTICIPANTS TO DRAW CONCLUSIONS

Refraining from joining the discussion and from advocating, elaborating, and defending your own views does not prevent you from helping people to *draw conclusions* and *make decisions.* For example, in judicial fashion you can ask people what they make of the discussion thus far. Or you can nudge them towards conclusions in Socratic fashion by asking leading questions about the *implications* of their views. "If what you say is true, George, about the rocky road of political reform, and also what you say, Ann, about impatience for quick economic results, then isn't antidemocratic backlash a distinct possibility in countries that are breaking away from one-party rule?" Alternatively, you can ask people questions about their *assumptions*. "You seem to be saying, both of you, that socialism necessarily means that the government owns everything. How would you describe Sweden, where far more production is in private hands than in many other countries?" Drawing people out in this way sharpens their thinking not only when they are looking for closure but also when they are looking to expand their inquiries.

Choosing a Leadership Role

You always guide a discussion, so, to choose a leadership role or combination of roles is to say what *priority* you want to assign to the tasks of controlling the discussion, joining the discussion, and helping others draw conclusions.

In choosing from among the six basic leadership roles outlined below, keep in mind the following questions:

- How *formally* and *closely* do you want to control the discussion?

- How *fully* do you you want to participate in it?

- How *strongly* do you want to intervene to help people draw conclusions and reach decisions?

Listed in descending order of control, the discussion-leader roles we invite you to consider are the *directive* role, the *influential* role, the *persuasive* role, the *instructional* role, the *facilitative* role, and the *collegial* role.

DIRECTIVE

The directive role requires that you establish and follow an agenda, observe protocol, and maintain a high degree of impartiality. Though you don't have to observe strict parliamentary procedure, you do have to ensure that discussion and debate proceed in an orderly manner and that everyone is given a fair hearing. The standard reference manual for such meetings is *Robert's Rules of Order,* which stipulates precise procedures for making motions, conducting and ending debate, making amendments, postponements, and voting. If you are in a position of senior responsibility, it behooves you to familiarize yourself with *Robert's Rules,* less to be able to direct a discussion rigidly than to be able to resolve conflicts when they arise. How many people realize, for example, that according to accepted rules, a motion to adjourn can only be voted on, not debated, or that the motion to reconsider a valid subject of debate cannot be amended? If participants agree to abide by *Robert's Rules* as necessary, you can make good use of them to avoid hemming and hawing about issues tangential to the purpose of the meeting.

Armed with *Robert's Rules,* you can closely control the *format* of the meeting, including the reaching of conclusions and the making of decisions; however, the *substance* of the meeting is in the hands of the participants. Your role is like that of the conductor of an orchestra: you may shape and direct the performance; but you do not, *ever,* wrench an instrument from the hands of a player and say, "No, do it this way, you fool!" Not even Toscanini could get away with that.

INFLUENTIAL

An influential role is perhaps the most common role for senior people to adopt when conducting a discussion. You select and schedule topics for discussion but don't usually concern yourself with strict protocol and formal procedure. You influence both the content and the outcome of inquiry, because you are respected for your knowledge, expertise, authority, or demonstrated ability to help people do a good job. You *run* the discussion and *participate* in it from time to time, principally when matters of policy arise. For example, as dean, chief scientist, department head, or CEO, you speak for the long-term interests of your organization and advise people about its goals, plans, and resources. You also help participants to reach conclusions and decisions by drawing them out on the assumptions and implications of what they say or do *not* say. For example, "Fred, there's no doubt that we would all like to see expansion in the marketing division, but has your committee considered how to allocate more resources to it without causing problems elsewhere?" Or, "Is the development of a graduate concentration in music education consistent with the primary goal of this conservatory to train professional musicians? How would such a program fit in here?"

As an influential leader, you carry on a mental dialogue with participants, silently posing important questions to them. When nobody raises those questions, *then* you intervene, alerting the participants to the questions, issues, or evidence they need to consider. In this manner, you influence the outcome of inquiry without determining exactly what the outcome will be, for you want people to *own* their conclusions and decisions.

PERSUASIVE

In the persuasive role, you have a case to make. You control the discussion long enough to make your case, but *no longer*. After you have made your case, you step back. Instead of continuing to control the discussion, you now guide it and participate in it as appropriate, to defend your case and assist in evaluating it.

When you assume the persuasive role, you aim to convince people to come to a *particular conclusion.* Very importantly, however, you do *not* engage in an adversary proceeding. You do not seek to *win* at the expense of truth and public benefit. You do not resort to debating tricks and parliamentary manuevers; rather, you participate objectively in testing your case.

INSTRUCTIONAL

In the instructional role you help participants master a process of reflection and disciplined thinking, enabling them to draw distinctions, understand technicalities, and assess evidence appropriate to a particular subject matter. You elucidate the *standards* of objectivity and inquiry peculiar to a discipline or subject area. You don't attempt to think *for* the student but rather try to draw the student into a way of thinking by asking leading questions. For example, "What would you make of these facts?" "Remember the first explanation we came up with? Does it still work?" "Given these conditions, why wouldn't you do exactly what this group of people did?"

Such educating is a delicate art requiring confidence in your grasp of a subject combined with sufficient humility to withstand criticism and challenges from all quarters. By humility we mean acknowledging with dignity and patience that you could be wrong on any given point. As an educator, one of your key tasks is to *make it safe* for people, including yourself, to be wrong and to make mistakes. Mistakes you regard as *information,* not as mortal sins. Objections you regard as *questions* for discussion, not as personal attacks.

Instructional leadership usually requires a detailed discussion plan, including a schedule of topics to be covered. But you don't follow such plans slavishly, turning a discussion into a lecture. Because you know your subject well, you can easily and spontaneously depart from your plan to follow a promising line of inquiry or to help people out of difficulties.

FACILITATIVE

The facilitative role is the role of the moderator, the honorary chair, the unobtrusive interviewer, the person who guides but does not control strictly or participate extensively. You make sure that everyone gets equal opportunity to speak. For example, if someone is dominating the discussion, then your job is to cut in: "I'm sorry, Mr. Cluck, Mr. Quack has been trying to get a word in here for several minutes." You also queue up speakers from the floor in the order in which they raised their hands during an open-discussion period: "I believe you, sir, were first, then you, madam, then you, down there in front." Again, if speakers get too long-winded, you intervene politely but forcefully: "Sir, you seem to be making a speech rather than asking a question. Could you please ask a question of a member of the panel?"

Facilitative leaders are often as well informed as the participants in a discussion, but theirs is the task of drawing out the views of others, not of presenting their own views. Television interviewers are adept at the game. "But what will Israel's military policy be, Prime Minister? What do you think, Mr. Chairman?"

COLLEGIAL

The collegial discussion leader is a first among equals. You organize the discussion of a subject so people can follow your thinking, and you theirs, but without tight scheduling or formal control. If you want to present your own views on the subject, you submit them for discussion rather than argue for them. As a collegial leader, you help others draw conclusions and distinctions in the Socratic way, by asking leading questions, but also as a full participant. For example, "Fred, my evidence shows that metamorphic activity was widely prevalent on the fringes of the central volcanic cone in the Bay of Fundy. Have you seen these samples? What do you think of them?" Or, "I'd appreciate your comments on this interpretation of the data. . . ." Here, the discussion is governed primarily by the criteria of rationality, argumentation, evidence, and testing peculiar to the field in which the participants are working. In short, *the collegial leader plays a nominal leadership role in an exchange between peers.*

Questions to Be Considered

Consider the following questions when choosing a leadership role.

- Will you be expected to play the same role throughout the discussion, or will you be able to shift from one role to another, for instance from the influential to the instructional, from the instructional to the persuasive?

- What do you want to accomplish in this discussion? What do the participants want to accomplish? How would you like to contribute? By getting your views across to them? By assessing their views? By promoting better understanding among the participants? By getting them to reach a particular decision or conclusion, or *any* decision or conclusion, or none?

- Is the discussion open-ended and continuing, or is closure on some issue or action expected? (Remember, the more open-ended the discussion, the less formal control required, as in the collegial or instructional roles.)

- How important will emotional and political factors be? How "hot" are the issues to be discussed? How are people likely to behave? Constructively, by addressing the issues on their merits? Or obstructively, by trying to defeat or to appease each other? If the latter, more control of the meeting is likely required.

Role-play the discussion in your imagination. Rehearse one role in your mind, then another, visualizing what will likely happen. Then, choose the role or the combination of roles you like best.

CHAPTER 4

Preparing a Discussion Plan

BASIC DISCUSSION PLANS

Discussion plans help you manage inquiry as an organized collective process, sometimes by giving general direction, sometimes by exercising tight control. Let's look at examples of basic plans.

First suppose yourself to be leading a general meeting of members of a citizens group who want to learn what's been happening in your city and what your city government has been doing about it. Your plan for the meeting provides for opening remarks and includes a list of topics and a set of questions about them:

1. Opening Remarks

2. Topics
   - Multicultural work force
   - Neighborhood economic development
   - University expansion

3. Questions
   - Who's doing what? When? Why? Where?

- To whom? For whom and with whom?
- Who wins? Who loses? Who cares?

Having informed themselves, the members of your group call another meeting to discuss issues with city councillors whom they helped to elect. You announce the following plan for the second meeting:

1. Opening remarks

2. Topics
   - Accomplishments
   - Support we've given councillors
   - Support they've given us
   - Improving communication

3. Questions
   - What results have been achieved and how do we/they feel about them?
   - How and how well have councillors responded to our concerns and issues?
   - How and how well have we responded to the needs of councillors?
   - How and how well have we been communicating with councillors and they with us, and how can we do better?

Now suppose you're a student of economics planning a scholarly discussion of option-pricing theory for a seminar that you hope will result in a significant contribution to knowledge. To enable yourself to determine how best to open discussion on the matter, you've developed four models for leading the discussion. Here are the models you're considering.

Model 1

In Model 1, you open by questioning the *adequacy* of current option-pricing theory.

1. Introduction
   - What major claims does current option-pricing theory make?
   - What strengths and weaknesses do we find in that theory?

2. Discussion
   - Can we modify current theory successfully, or do we need a better theory?
   - What would a better theory have to explain?

Model 2

Changing your first two questions slightly, you open in Model 2 by questioning the *validity* of current theory.

1. Introduction
   - According to current theory, what should we expect to observe?
   - What are we actually observing?

2. Discussion
   - Can we modify current theory successfully, or do we need a better theory?
   - What would a better theory have to explain?

Model 3

Shifting your initial focus from theory to data, you open in Model 3 by calling attention to *obvious anomalies,* that is, to phenomena that are generally known to require explanation yet resist it.

1. Introduction
   - What phenomena have we been observing?
   - Why have we found them so surprising?

2. Discussion
   - Can we modify current theory to explain them, or do we need a better theory?
   - What would a better theory have to explain?

Model 4

Finally, changing your first two questions slightly, you open in Model 4 by calling attention to *previously unnoticed anomalies,* that is, to phenomena just now coming to notice that require yet resist explanation.

1. Introduction
   - What kinds of observations were we accustomed to record?
   - What kinds of observations do we now find ourselves making?

2. Discussion
   - Can we modify current theory to explain these new observations, or do we need a better theory?
   - What would a better theory have to explain?*

The above examples show how you prepare a basic discussion plan: first, you provide for brief introductory remarks to focus attention on the subject, arouse interest, supply any needed background information, and perhaps explain ground rules; second, if you're going to be talking about several subjects or several aspects of a complex subject, you provide for introducing them in logical order. Third, you present the major questions you'll ask participants to ensure they address the issues

---

*For the theory underlying the four examples, see Kinneavy's "The Logic of Exploratory Discourse" in *A Theory of Discourse* (Kinneavy 1980, pp. 141–146).

you want to raise and consider the factors you deem relevant.

DETAILED DISCUSSION PLANS

A basic discussion plan consisting of introductory remarks, a list of topics, and a list of major questions suffices for discussion of many subjects under many varied circumstances. A basic plan can also suffice for discussions of complex subjects when people know their subject and know what's expected of them. For example, as a member of your citizens group, you know that people coming to your meetings expect to follow a democratic procedure modeled on *Robert's Rules of Order.* As a scholar in economics, you know that people coming to your seminar expect to observe the canons and guidelines of that discipline when offering and judging evidence and argument.

But a basic discussion plan will likely not suffice when people lack a canon or guidelines for discussion of such complex subjects as goals and action plans, explored in Chapters Five and Six, or when your purpose includes helping people reach some kind of closure. Then you'll need a detailed plan. Depending on the leadership role you've chosen, that plan should probably include one or more of the following additional elements:

- Supplementary questions to be asked after each major question, to bring it into sharper focus, elicit different opinions, and encourage all participants to contribute

- Questions to test for agreement on each major question, as appropriate, enabling you to summarize, move on to the next major question, and build to a conclusion

- Provision for interim and final summaries of remarks you expect to make or expect others to make, and provision for drawing conclusions you expect to reach or expect others to reach

- Provision for sharing your knowledge and experience with others, for expressing and defending your opinions, and for challenging the opinions of others

Detailed discussion plans can be modeled on a type of manual called a leader's guide or instructor's guide. These guides are often used by executives and managers to run seminars and conduct training programs. Somebody whose job or business is "training and development" or "human resource development" can show you such manuals. What you'll find in them is likely to remind you of stage directions or lesson plans.

SOCIAL AND POLITICAL ISSUES

Always an intellectual process, inquiry is often a significantly emotional and political process as well. To complete your plan, ask yourself what social and political issues the discussion is likely to raise: What issues of social and economic well-being? Of self-esteem and self-determination? Of pride, power, position, and privilege? What issues of little importance? Of moderate importance? Of great importance? What issues of importance to participants? Of importance to *you?* What issues that you want to address? That you want to avoid? That you *cannot* avoid?

Expect problems to arise if people are going to encounter significant emotional and political issues. Very likely, they won't be able to work together effectively without your help. Fearing to express or arouse strong feelings, they'll refuse to raise or address critical questions. Or fearing they'll come to harm, they'll perceive others as intending to hurt them. The participants are also unlikely to be able to address the subject productively. If they regard the others as friends to be retained, they'll decline to challenge the others' ideas; instead, they'll agree with the others, seeking not wisdom but to keep the peace. Or if they regard the others as enemies to be defeated, they'll refuse to listen to them; instead, they'll attack them, seeking not wisdom but to get their own way.

If you expect such problems, you may want your plan to include a special provision for creating and maintaining a climate conducive to inquiry. For example, to avoid a destructive, adversarial proceeding, you may want to begin discussion by helping people establish common ground. If that's the kind of special provision you want to make, you'll benefit by consulting two products of the Harvard Negotiation Project, *Getting to Yes* (Fisher and Ury 1983) and *Getting Together* (Fisher and Brown 1989). Likewise, to help people make sound decisions, you may want to begin by gaining their agreement to consider key questions they would otherwise probably want to avoid. If that's the kind of special provision you want to make, we recommend *Reasoning, Learning and Action* by Chris Argyris of the Harvard Graduate School of Business Administration (Argyris 1983). See also *Getting Past No: Negotiating with Difficult People* (Ury 1991).

Techniques for making decisions under difficult circumstances are described in *The Compleat Problem Solver,* Part III (Hayes 1989). All of Part III may be read with profit.

SUMMARY AND CHECKLISTS

Let's summarize, first giving you a checklist for preparing a basic plan of inquiry, then a checklist for preparing a detailed plan.

Checklist for Preparing a Basic Discussion Plan

1. Provide for brief introductory remarks to focus attention on the subject, arouse interest, supply any needed background information, and perhaps explain ground rules.

2. If you're going to be talking about several subjects or several aspects of a complex subject, provide for introducing them in logical order.

3. Record the major questions you'll ask to ensure that participants address the issues you want to raise and consider the factors you deem relevant.

If a basic plan of inquiry will suffice, you're now ready to issue a call for your meeting. In Chapter Eight, you'll find an exploration of the intellectual, emotional, political, practical, and logistical issues involved in issuing that call.

Checklist for Preparing a Detailed Discussion Plan

Of course, a basic plan may not suffice. Maybe you're going to be discussing a complex subject with people who aren't familiar with the recognized canon or guidelines for the field of inquiry; for example, the canon for an inquest or the guidelines for administrative hearings. Or maybe a recognized canon is lacking for the subject, as with the subject of goals or the subject of problems. Under such circumstances, you'll probably want to prepare a detailed plan that involves one or more of the following additional steps.

4. Record supplementary questions to be asked after each major question, to bring it into sharper focus, elicit different opinions, and encourage all participants to contribute.

5. Record supplementary questions that you can use to test for agreement on each major question, as appropriate, enabling you to summarize, move on to the next major question, and build to a conclusion.

6. Provide for interim reviews and final summaries that you expect to make or expect others to make, and provide for drawing conclusions that you expect to reach or expect others to reach.

7. Provide for sharing your knowledge and experience with others, for expressing and defending your opinions, and for challenging the opinions of others.

Finally, when important social and political issues are likely to arise, you may want to make special provision for avoiding problems and maintaining a climate conducive to inquiry.

CHAPTER 5

Analyzing Situations and Setting Goals

Over the years, nearly every business meeting we've ever attended in the public, private, and nonprofit sectors has in some way concerned the five subjects we're about to explore in this and the next two chapters—*analyzing situations, setting goals, making plans, evaluating plans,* and *identifying the causes of problems.* We'll share with you what we've learned about guiding productive discussions of those subjects. What we've learned comes not only from our own experience but also from the experience of masters whom we've been privileged to work with and study. For your consideration, we'll be offering guidelines in key areas of inquiry where no recognized canons exist, attempting to codify the best of what we've seen and heard. We'll also refer you to selected published sources.

To illustrate our recommended approaches for discussing situations, goals, plans, and problems, we've drawn heavily on our experience in business and in economic development because it's easy to talk about measurable and observable results in those fields. But please don't conclude from our business and economic examples that you can't or shouldn't consider using our recommended approaches for a wide variety of purposes. Indeed, one of the authors has used this chapter and following chapters in a course intended to help people use writing to manage their practical business affairs, only to discover that some of his students were using his recommended goal-setting process to plan short stories, design scientific reports and prepare graduate papers on moral and theological questions.

Accordingly, we think that what follows is of value to you, whoever you are, whatever you may be doing, and wherever you may want to go. We invite you to familiarize yourself with Chapters Five, Six, and Seven as resources to which you can return when, for example, you're getting ready to talk about goals, or while you're already talking about them, or while you're getting ready to talk about plans, or while you're already helping others to think about them.

Narrowly considered, Chapters Five, Six, and Seven are *guides* to be used when needed while preparing discussion plans (see Chapter Four) and while calling for discussion and conducting discussion (see Chapters Eight and Nine). Structures of discussion are presented, questions for discussion are suggested, rationales for the structures and questions are described.

Absent any immediate need to think about situations and goals and plans and problems, you may want to scan this and the next two chapters on your way to Chapter Eight; however, if you take the time to familiarize yourself with the contents of Chapters Five, Six, and Seven, you may find that, broadly considered, they describe a *management process* that you and others can use from day to day.

ANALYZING SITUATIONS

Situation analyses are *discussions of events and conditions that affect our interests and require a response.* Typically, we ask ourselves (1) what's going on and (2) what we ought to do about it. Often, we should first ask ourselves (3) what we *ought to talk about* and what we *ought to know about it.*

By nature, situation analyses are *deliberative, not directive:* we want to *learn* what's happening and *decide* what to do, rather than be *told* what's happening and then *sold* the decisions of others.

Coming to a briefing rather than a discussion, we expect our leaders to sell us a response of their own making. We expect them to present their findings, conclusions, and recommendations for action, or their goals and their plans for achieving those goals. We expect them to say what they want us to think and do; therefore, we also expect them to present their data *selectively*—for the purpose of persuading us to place our confidence in their judgment.

Coming to a discussion, we expect our leaders to guide us toward a response of our own making, and to place *their* confidence in *our* judgment. We expect them to present data *inclusively*—all the data required to give us strong faith in our understanding of the situation and also in our ability to identify and weigh choices for changing it.

Attending a briefing, we want to evaluate the product of a thought process, not participate in a learning process. We expect our leaders to tell us *only* what they believe is critical or important for us to know. Attending a discussion, we want to determine for ourselves what is critical and important; therefore, we want *all* data that may be relevant to our concerns.

Discussing What's Going On

A discussion of *what's going on* can be built on the following first set of questions, stated as they might be put to a group that you're leading:

- What events and conditions are affecting our interests or are likely to affect them?

- What opportunities does the situation give us?

- What threats does the situation present?

- What strengths could give us an advantage?

- What weaknesses could put us at a disadvantage?

Threats and *opportunities* are current or future *events:* They represent things that you either *don't* want to happen or *do* want to happen. *Strengths* and *weaknesses* are current or future *conditions.* They represent the presence or absence of things that you need in order to counter threats and to seize or create opportunities.

Suppose you're discussing factors affecting the economy of a semirural tri-state region. Your *threats* might include "growing absentee ownership of major enterprises," and your *opportunities,* "development of hydroelectric power." Your *strengths* might include "attractive residential areas," and your *weaknesses,* "inadequate local tax revenues."

Discussing What We Ought to Do About It

A discussion of *what we ought to do* about what's going on can be built on the following set of questions, also stated as they might be put to a group that you're leading:

- What opportunities should we take to *advance* our interests?

- What threats should we counter to *protect* our interests?

- How should we *maximize* our strengths, and *preserve* or *increase* them?

- How should we *minimize* our weaknesses, and *eliminate* or *reduce* them?

- What *options* should we consider as *responses* to the situation?

When you first ask these questions, you're likely to get vague answers. For example, if your *threats* include absentee ownership, then people may propose to counter that threat by "encouraging local entrepreneurs." And, if your *opportunities* include hydroelectric power, then people may propose to "finance a dam."

As discussion proceeds, you should ask people to present increasingly concrete proposals for action, stating them as *simple* options or as *complex* options, and describing them with varying degrees of specificity.

SIMPLE OPTIONS

Suppose you've been discussing the competitive status and performance of your company's products. Suppose also that you can safely predict the costs, benefits, and consequences of your company's actions. In such a situation, you can ask people to state their options straightforwardly as *strategies, programs,* or *goals* that commit them to act.

Here's a proposed strategy describing *what we ought*

to do in very general terms, and serving as a *mandate* for action:

> Develop new products to strengthen our current market position.

Here's a proposed program identifying steps consistent with your strategy, and serving as a *guide* to action:

> Develop product A, product B, and product C to strengthen our market position.

And here's a proposed goal describing *what we ought to do* in highly measurable terms, and serving as a *call* to action:

> Begin national introduction of product A on June 30, fully supported by national advertising . . .

COMPLEX OPTIONS

Suppose you're analyzing a complicated military, diplomatic, competitive, or political situation in which you *cannot* safely predict the costs, benefits, and consequences of your actions. In such a situation, you can state your choices cautiously in the form of scenarios that suggest what you ought to do without committing yourself to doing it.

In the following example, you've identified the actions *they* might take in response to the actions *we* might take:

	We might		*They might*
A.	. . . .	X.	. . . .
B.	. . . .	Y.	. . . .
C.	. . . .	Z.	. . . .

You also might want to identify what *they* might do if *we* were to exercise a particular option; and what *we* might do if *they* were to exercise a particular option; and what might happen then, to *us* and to *them*. For example:

If we . . .	*If they . . .*
Do A, they might do B, with result 1.	Do C, we might do D, with result 2.
Do E, they might do F, with result 3.	Do G, we might do H, with result 4.

You should always consider the possibility that maybe *what we ought to do* is *nothing*. As alternatives to simple options and complex options alike, consider options to take *no* action or to to make *no* change in present plans. For example, extend the above list to include the following:

If we . . .	*If they . . .*
Don't do I, they might do J, with result 5.	Do K, we might **not** do L, with result 6.

Generating Options

You can use two methods to generate your options: the Method of Judgment and the Method of Imagination. When you follow the Method of Judgment, you develop options by *drawing lessons* from experience, and you *evaluate* your options by *applying well-defined standards* of efficiency and effectiveness. By contrast, when you follow the Method of Imagination, you *suspend judgment* because you want to prevent your experience of the past from limiting your thinking about the present and the future.

THE METHOD OF JUDGMENT

Do the following to employ the Method of Judgment:

- Consider how you've handled similar situations before. Ask yourself *what worked* for you and *what didn't.*

- Consider how others have handled similar situations. *What worked* for them and *what didn't?*

- Propose strategies, goals, and programs to serve your interests in the current situation.

- Evaluate your proposals against standards for:
  - (*a*) *efficient use* of resources, and especially for use of scarce, irreplaceable, or expensive resources
  - (*b*) *effective delivery* of benefits, especially for delivery of significant benefits.
  - (*c*) *effective control* of costs, and especially for control of significant costs.

To develop standards, you can ask people to describe evidence for success. What will happen? When will it happen? How will they know that it's happened? You can also ask people to name the proposals they consider good, better, and best, and then to defend their choices. By what standards are they making their choices? By what measures of success are the better proposals superior to the good, and the best proposals superior to the better?

THE METHOD OF IMAGINATION

Do the following to employ the Method of Imagination:

- Search your experience and that of others for ideas about strategies, goals, and programs, not limiting yourself to thinking about situations that are similar to the one you're discussing.

- Evaluate *none* of those ideas about strategies, goals, and programs. Instead, welcome *all* ideas and reject *none,* praise *all* ideas and criticize *none.*

- Now consider similar situations that you and others have faced. *Disregard* what was *actually* done; instead, answer the following questions:
  (*a*) What *could* have been done in those *past* situations, assuming unlimited support? Unlimited time? Unlimited resources?
  (*b*) What could have been done differently? Better? For the first time?

- Now consider the current situation, and answer the following questions:
  (*a*) What could be done in the present situation, assuming unlimited support? Time? Resources?
  (*b*) What could now be done differently? Better? For the first time?

- Review every step you've thought of taking, however serious or frivolous, asking yourself what would happen if you did it, and what would happen if you didn't do it.

THE METHODS OF JUDGMENT AND IMAGINATION COMPARED

Strong attacks have been made on the Method of Judgment by students of decision making who fear the closed mind as friendly to few ideas and as hostile to new ideas. In reply, proponents of the Method of Judgment attack the Method of Imagination as whimsical, trendy, and subjective. Still other students of decision making report that people who rely on either method can develop equally good ideas with equal effort in equal time.

Those other students of decision making also report that inspiration comes to those who seek it methodically, consciously informing imagination with judgment, joining native powers of association—their native powers to associate like with like—to their acquired power to separate good from bad. In sum, success in developing good ideas appears to result frequently from a *conscious effort* to develop good ideas—an effort that includes:

- identifying and defining standards of efficiency and effectiveness

- employing judgment consciously, for the purpose of informing imagination with judgment

- employing imagination freely

- welcoming inspiration, but not waiting for it

For an extended discussion of the merits of judgment and imagination, see David Perkins's *The Mind's Best Work* (Perkins 1981), to which we owe much.

Starting with the Right Information

Often, before asking ourselves what's going on and what we ought to do about it, we should first ask ourselves *what we ought to talk about* and *what we ought to know about it.* In other words, we should first talk about getting the kind of information that will help us make wise decisions.

Here's a series of questions we can ask ourselves to design research that will get us that kind of information:

- What do we expect of ourselves, and what do others expect of us, as reflected, for example, in our missions, strategies, programs, goals, duties, and activities?

- What threats and opportunities and strengths and weaknesses do we think we'll discover when we study the situation?

- What options are we likely to propose? What new or revised missions, strategies, programs, goals, duties, and activities?

- What *types* of data will show whether our projected threats and opportunities and strengths and weaknesses exist, and also show how important they are?

- What *depth* of data will show whether the threats and opportunities and strengths and weaknesses exist, and also show how important they are?

- What *types* and *depth* of data will we need to evaluate the options that we're likely to propose?

Existing research designs may meet our needs or serve as the basis for discussion. For example, suppose we want to discuss how best to further the economic development of our region of the country. Consider Exhibit 1, which presents a sample of the types of data deemed relevant by an economic-development agency.

Exhibit 1

Factors Affecting Regional Economic Development

A. Describe the relationship between the economic status of the community and the social well-being of the community, as reflected by the following indicators:
  - average family incomes
  - unemployment rates
  - mortgage foreclosure rates
  - net emigration of skilled labor, young people, and college-educated residents
  - expenditures on welfare
  - expenditures on education
  - nature and extent of public services and facilities

B. Identify and appraise the basic economic resources of the community:
  - Identify and describe the community's natural resources, labor resources, and capital resources.
  - Describe the current and potential utilization of those resources.
  - Describe location factors, including roads and transportation, community facilities, energy sources, economic overheads, and the nature of demand.
  - Distinguish between factors subject to com-

munity influence and factors not subject to community influence.
- Differentiate between problems caused primarily by impersonal market forces and problems caused primarily by personal choice in both the public sector and the private sector.

Or suppose we want to discuss how best to strengthen our position in the market by introducing new products. Consider Exhibit 2, which presents a sample of the data deemed relevant by a group of professional advisers to small businesses.

Exhibit 2

Market Research and Evaluation Data

A. Customers
   - Identify and classify potential customers by major market segment.
   - Name the potential customers in each market segment, and identify their principal places of business.
   - Describe the relative importance of the following to purchase decisions by major potential customers: price, quality, service, personal contact, political pressures.
   - Name potential customers who have expressed interest in the proposed product or service. Explain the reasons for their interest.
   - Name potential customers who have shown no interest and explain why. Also explain how you will arouse their interest.
B. Competition
   - Compare competing products or services on the basis of price, performance, service, warranties, and other pertinent features.

- Discuss the current advantages and disadvantages of competing products and services. Describe how well these products and services are meeting the needs of customers.
- Identify the managerial strengths and weaknesses of competing companies.
- Provide data on other companies' market shares and sales, their distribution and production capabilities, and their current, historical, and projected profitability.
- Identify the pricing leader and the quality leader.
- Name companies which have entered or left the market in recent years. Explain why they have done so.
- Explain why customers now buy from your leading prospective competitors.
- Describe how you will win their customers.

Existing research designs should all be evaluated carefully. Most will need revision: in their present condition, some will be incomplete and others inappropriate. For example, consider the existing design for economic-development research, presented above as Exhibit 1. Will that design serve our purposes? Not if we care who benefits from development. The existing design calls only for data on average family income, not for data on the distribution of income by age, race, and gender. Unaware of distribution, and hence ignorant of groups whose incomes are low, we cannot plan for improvement in their economic well-being.

Consider, too, the existing design for market research, presented above as Exhibit 2. No questions are asked about people. What qualifications are required to sell our products effectively? Where can qualified people be found? What type and level of compensation will qualified people want?

SETTING GOALS

A goal is a statement of intent to create value and to prove you've created it by meeting clear standards of performance, standards that define the meaning of success. Here are some basic questions to discuss when you want to define that meaning:

- How much of what kind of value do you intend to create?

- Who will benefit from creation of this value? How? When? Where?

- How can you best demonstrate that you've succeeded in creating this value?

In this section of Chapter Five, we'll explore the intellectual process of constructing the meaning of success, including its meaning as measurable results, as observable results, as improved results, and as qualified results.

Goals for Measurable Results

Suppose you sell for a manufacturer of consumer goods. Your company has just announced a new product. Your boss has just asked you to set a goal for placing it with the chain stores you serve. You draft the following goal for a key account:

Place new product with Key Account by May 15.

Here's how you and your boss might engage in the process of refining that goal.

"Does that goal say what you want?" she asks. "If that's what you want, you could get it by convincing Key Account to put just one sample of our new product on just one shelf in just one of their stores. Tell me what you mean by the words you're using. What do you mean by *place new product?*"

You begin by saying you'll define *new product* as a quantity of one thousand dozen.

"Good," says the boss. "Now, what sizes do you have in mind? Sixteen-ounce? Twelve-ounce? Eight-ounce?" You reply that you first want to define what you mean by *place with Key Account.*

Key Account is a chain store. Ideally, you'd like to achieve wide distribution for the new product; that is, you'd like to convince Key Account to offer the new product throughout the chain, in each and every store. But Key Account isn't likely to put a new product into any stores except its largest ones, classified as *A* stores. Moreover, the management of *each* of those stores can accept or reject recommendations from headquarters about carrying a new product; therefore, you decide to try for eight of the company's ten *A* stores.

You revise your draft goal to read as follows:

> Place 1,000 dozen new product in 80% of Key Account's *A* stores by May 15.

"Great," says your boss. "Now we need to know what you mean by saying *place one thousand dozen by May 15.* Do you mean that Key Account approves the purchase? That Key Account signs an order? That the company's warehouse receives one thousand dozen? That the store managers place their orders with the warehouse? That clerks put the product on the shelves?"

Your boss is asking important questions, for the company buys by committee. Here are the steps in the process: First you have to sell your new product to the buyer who handles your type of merchandise. The buyer than presents a proposed overall company order to the Buying Committee at its weekly meeting. If the Buying Committee recommends the new product and accepts the buyer's proposed order, then the company lists the new product in a weekly circular sent to its store managers during the following week. The store managers then place their orders with the company's warehouse, using a form included in the circular.

You decide that *place by May 15* will mean that store managers take delivery of one thousand dozen and display the new product on end-aisle stands. In other words, *place* will mean that Key Account's stores are *offering* the product to the public, not simply that Key Account is recommending the new product to its store managers.

You tell your boss that *place* will mean "on display." She now asks you about sales promotion for the new product. You reply that you'll cover sales promotion in your plan for achieving your goal. In describing your tasks, you'll show that Key Account's stores will run local newspaper ads for the new product on May 15, following the beginning of your company's national advertising campaign. Your *plan* will show in detail what your *goal* means.

You now argue that you've set a workable, well-defined goal. True, you haven't specified what sizes of the new product you want to place. But you're supposed to be writing a goal, not a fully detailed sales order. True, you haven't said what quantities you want to put on the shelves of each store. But you're supposed to be writing a goal, not a fully detailed selling plan. And true, your overall quantity of one thousand dozen is subject to question, because you haven't conducted the research into product movement that precedes the preparation of a selling plan; therefore, you don't know how well Key Account has performed with comparable new products in the past. But your experience tells you that one thousand dozen is a reasonable target for the present. Your experience also tells you that you can realistically expect a favorable response from eight out of ten managers of *A* stores.

Your boss agrees that you and she have described highly measurable results. She now asks whether you and she will be happy with those results. In other words, does the goal truly describe value that you and she want to create? How will achieving that goal benefit the people you both want to benefit?

You realize that the goal does *not* truly describe value that you and she want to create. As a statement of intent to create value, your goal is incomplete, for you've only said that you want to *sell in,* that is, that you want to sell the new product to *Key Account.* You haven't said that you want to *sell through*—that you want to help Key Account move the new product off its shelves and into the hands of consumers through effective retail advertising, pricing, and display.

If the new product doesn't sell through, then at minimum Key Account will have wasted its money. In addition, consumers will have lost opportunity to make use of your new product. Plus, your company will have lost opportunity to build its business. Indeed, if the new product doesn't sell through, then you've defeated the whole purpose of introducing a new product; you've achieved a one-shot sale of a new product, but you've failed to create a market for it.

To make sure that *place* means "create a market," your boss might well ask you to set two coordinated goals, one for sell-in and the other for sell-through. For example:

> Place 1,000 dozen new product in Key Account
> *A* stores by May 15, and sell through initial order
> by August 1.

You could argue that any sensible seller would obviously want to present an effective plan for selling through as means for selling in, and that any sensible buyer would obviously want to follow such a plan. So why call for sell-through by name?

We'd reply that calling for the obvious by name can help sensible people avoid serious errors of omission, errors they can easily make if everyone assumes that to *mean* well is to *do* good.

Goals for Observable Results

Suppose your company has established a priority for "improving communication," so you draft the following goal for discussion with your boss:

> Conduct effective business meetings to improve
> communication during the second half of the year.

Your boss begins by asking what you think the management is looking for: What's going to make them happy? What's going to give the management reason to believe that "communication" among the employees is improving? You reply, "People will trust each other more. They'll understand the company's problems better. They'll show a greater commitment to the company's success."

"Okay," says your boss. "Let's try to define *effective business meetings* in terms of those kinds of results. What would *you* be happy to see and hear? What would give *you* reason to believe that people were trusting each other more?"

You reply, "For one thing, people could take the risk

of admitting to mistakes publicly rather than try to cover them up, so we could fix things fast before they turn into disasters."

"That would sure be a good sign," your boss says. "What other kinds of risks might people take in your meetings or after your meetings, to show that they trusted each other?"

You reply, "They could ask for help or accept help, not act like other people who could help them were trying to make them look bad."

"That gives us two good examples of the kind of results we're looking for," says your boss. "And I think we ought to go with representative examples because there isn't any one definitive way that people are going to show that they trust each other."

In other words, you might want to set your goal by describing the types of things people will do. For example:

> Conduct effective business meetings during the second half of the year, with results like the following to show we're communicating better.
> • People will call attention to their own mistakes in time for corrective action to be taken.
> • People will freely ask for help and accept help. . . .

Describing what people will *do* is the key to setting goals of many kinds. For example, here's a goal to create value in the form of technical skill and knowledge:

> Acquire and demonstrate the ability to read financial statements by September 30, specifically including the ability to
> • compare cash flows
> • evaluate credit risks
> • derive the current ratio . . .

And here's a goal to create value in the form of personal maturity and strength of character:

> Develop and show the self-confidence to take part effectively in the upcoming merger talks, by
> • responding calmly to personal or emotional attacks
> • confronting and resolving conflicts on the basis of mutual benefit . . .

And here are the questions to address when you want to define success by describing what people will *do*:

• What will people do *differently,* do *better,* or do *for the first time?*

• By *when* will they do it, under *what* conditions, and *where* and *how?*

Success can often be defined just by answering those questions. For example, suppose your goal is to learn French. Envision yourself using your knowledge successfully, then ask yourself these questions: *What are you showing that you've learned?* The spoken language? The written language? Both the spoken and the written? *Where are you?* In Paris, in Marseilles, in Martinique or Montreal? On the boulevard, in the bistro, on the beach, or on the bourse? *What are you trying to do there?* Hail a taxi? Order a meal? Make friends? Or make a profit? *How do you know that you're succeeding?* What is happening? How are you responding to others? To their spoken language? To their written language? How are others responding to you? To your spoken language? To your written language?

By answering those questions, you can set a goal to

make useful application of the value you've created, thereby establishing that you've created it.

Goals for Measurable *and* Observable Results

Some goals *can* be defined and *should* be defined in terms of measurable results *and* observable results. Suppose you want to perform an opera. You can measure success by the number of tickets sold, the percentage of seats filled, the demand for tickets for your next performance, and also by calculating your operating income or recording donations to your opera company. But suppose you want to perform the opera to high standards of musical and dramatic quality. Then you can't set a goal to create measurable value alone, because you can't demonstrate success solely by creating it. For example, members of your audience may buy tickets solely to see the theater or to see themselves or to go to an opera because it's an opera. In other words, people who don't know anything about opera can fill your theater for reasons which have nothing to do with musical or dramatic quality.

Someone must *do* something that *necessarily* shows that you're meeting high standards. *Who* will do it? The singers, musicians, or technicians? The conductor, director, or producer? The sponsors, critics, or members of the audience? Or you yourself? And *what* will these people do that will show that you're succeeding? What will they perform and how? How will they respond and when?

Also, suppose you want to introduce a management report service. Success can be defined by units sold or by dollar sales, or by profit or by contribution to profit. But that may not be enough. You may want to acknowledge that success in creating measurable value for yourself depends heavily on success in creating observable value for your customers, because you aren't producing a commodity, purchased primarily on price, but a service, purchased primarily for the benefits it yields. Therefore, you may also want to set a goal for creation of use value—a goal to enable others to succeed, stated explicitly in terms of the actions you'll enable others to take.

Envision yourself introducing your service successfully. Who are your initial customers? Where are they? What are they doing that you've helped them to do? That they couldn't do before? That they couldn't do as well? What are you helping them to do that contributes significantly to their success? What are your initial customers saying or writing about your service? In what ways are they recommending it to others like themselves?

Goals for Improved Results

Goals for improved results should be goals to create a measurable or observable *increase in value,* specifying where necessary a measurable *degree* of increase or an observable *kind* of increase. For example, suppose your boss wants you to set a goal to

> Raise average key chain store order size to 500 dozen.

You reply that she's asking you to set a goal for a 25 percent increase in average order size. "I think that's too much," you say, suggesting that you set a goal to

> Raise average key chain store order size by 15%, from 400 dozen at the beginning of the year to 460 dozen by the end of the year.

Earlier, we gave an example of a goal for achieving observable results, namely,

> Develop and show the self-confidence to take part effectively in the upcoming merger talks, by
> - responding calmly to personal or emotional attacks
> - confronting and resolving conflicts on the basis of mutual benefit . . .

Here's how that goal could be restated as a goal to achieve an observable increase in value:

> Develop and show the *increased* self-confidence *necessary* to take part effectively in the upcoming merger talks, by
>
> - responding calmly to personal or emotional attacks (*rather than responding angrily*)
> - confronting and resolving conflicts on the basis of mutual benefit (*rather than avoiding unpleasant but important issues*) . . .

As you can see, the restated goal provides a basis for comparison.

Goals for Qualified Results

In their simplest form, goals are two-part statements of intent to cause a measurable or observable effect. First you say generally what you want to achieve, then you say specifically what you want to achieve. For example:

> Raise the quality of key chain store selling plans to a professional level, specifically ensuring that all sales presentations

- include persuasive analyses of data on . . .
- show understanding of customer business needs and profit objectives, especially such needs as . . . and objectives for . . .

Goals can also take a more complicated three-part form. First you say generally what results you want to achieve, then you say how you're going to achieve them, then you say specifically what results you want to achieve. For example:

> Raise the quality of key chain store selling plans to a professional level by conducting effective training at quarterly sales meetings, specifically ensuring that all sales presentations
> - include persuasive analyses of data on . . .
> - show understanding of customer business needs and profit objectives, especially such needs as . . . and objectives for . . .

Suppose you've drafted the three-part goal above. It represents a commitment to achieving results that you *can* achieve and also can *prove* that you've achieved, for you *can* improve the quality of key chain store selling plans *solely* by means of conducting effective training at quarterly sales meetings.

Now suppose you're discussing your goal with your boss. "What you've done so far sounds fine," says she. "But the reason you improve key chain store selling plans is to build sales to those stores. So why not say so?" She proposes you revise your goal as follows:

> *Improve quarterly sales performance* by raising the quality of key chain store selling plans.

The boss hasn't proposed you revise your goal. She's proposed you set a new goal that you can't achieve *solely* by raising the quality of key chain store selling plans. How should you respond?

You can offer to set a goal for *qualified* success, that is, a goal worded to limit your responsibility for results. The simplest way to set such a goal is to use the verbal formula *"contribute to."* For example:

> *Contribute to* improving quarterly sales performance by raising the quality of key chain store selling plans.

You can also set a goal for qualified success by using the verbal formula *"provided that"* to cover conditions beyond your control. For example:

> Improve quarterly sales performance by raising the quality of key chain store selling plans, *provided that* the following conditions obtain:
> - Your company offers attractive trade promotions.
> - The economy continues to improve.
> - Your company doesn't suddenly cut its ad budget.
> - Unemployment holds steady.

We hope that by proposing such wordy goals for qualified success you can show your boss the merit of your original goal. A goal should enable you to gather and focus your energy on achieving results, just as a lens enables you to gather and focus light from an object you want to see. A wordy goal diffuses energy just as a cloudy lens diffuses light. Prefer to take responsibility for unqualified success.*

---

*Much of what we've been saying about the *clarity of evidence* for success may have sounded familiar to readers of Robert F. Mager. If you don't know his work, we recommend you to *Preparing Instructional Objectives* (Mager, revised second edition, 1984) and to *Goal Analysis* (Mager, second edition, 1984).

CHAPTER 6

Making and Evaluating Action Plans

MAKING PLANS

"If you don't know where you're going, any road will take you there." So it is said.

Accordingly, if you want to accomplish anything, first you must set your goals; second, you must make your plans; and third, you must follow your plans. Otherwise you will act aimlessly; you will waste your time; you will either fail to accomplish anything or fail to achieve the results you want.

We argue that the accepted truth is a half-truth. The only way to learn where you want to go, and learn what road to take, is to start trying to get there; the only way to learn what you really want to do, and learn how much you can do, is to start trying to do it.

Yes, you benefit greatly by defining what you want to accomplish, by setting a clear and realistic goal.

But no, only if first you act can you ever expect to set such a goal—only if first you act, to test your understanding of reality, and to ground your goal firmly on accurate understanding. As a wise person once truly said, "To discover what is real, you must first try to change it."

The accepted truth, that first you must set your goal, may lead you to make a common and dangerous assumption, that once you have set a goal carefully, and have carefully developed plans to achieve it, then you need not change your goal or your plans—the assumption that to set a goal means that you understand reality clearly, and that you have pledged your honor to achieve the specified results, and that to fail to achieve those results, once you have set your goal, is to fail in the performance of your duty.

The Linear Model for Planning

Accepted truth encourages fixation by presenting an oversimplified *linear* model of the process of setting and achieving goals. Here's what that linear model calls for:

The Linear Model for Planning

Step 1. Set Goals
Step 2. Make Plans
Step 3. Take Action
Step 4. Evaluate Final Results

The linear model encourages you to fix your ends and your means, to set up an idol, to surrender control to an oracle who speaks once and for all time—who demands your commitment, who threatens you with failure. To prevent yourself from fixing your ends and your means, you can follow a *cyclical* model that enables you to learn from your experience, first by simulating the results of the actions you propose to take, and second, by studying the results of the actions that you actually take.

The Cyclical Model for Planning

Here's what the cyclical model calls for:

The Cyclical Model for Planning

1. Set Goals to Create Value
2. Make Plans to Achieve Goals
   - *Describe tasks and action steps,* saying who will do what by when, to whom, for whom and with whom, where and how; and calling for regular review of interim results and revision of goals and plans.
   - *Simulate results,* first predicting what will happen, including what will go right and go wrong, then revising goals and plans as needed.
3. Work Your Plans
   - *Perform tasks and take action steps.*
   - *Review interim results,* first determining what has happened, including what has gone right and what has gone wrong, then deciding what you've learned from experience, then revising your goals and plans as needed.
4. Continue to Work Your Plans
   - *Perform* your tasks and action steps.
   - *Review* interim results.
   - *Revise* your goals and plans as needed.
5. Continue . . .
6. Continue . . .
7. Evaluate Final Results

The cyclical model encourages you to take responsibility rather then surrender control, enables you to consult yourself and your experience repeatedly, and enables you to strengthen your commitment to your goals and plans. By following the cyclical model you can give yourself reasonable opportunity to enjoy a success worth achieving.

To give yourself that opportunity, you should first develop a workable plan by describing tasks and action steps, simulating results, and revising goals and plans as needed. We recommend you develop that plan by addressing the four groups of basic questions presented below. After developing a workable plan, you should then evaluate it (see "Evaluating Plans," later in this chapter).

The Four Groups of Basic Questions
The four groups of basic questions to consider are *action, resource, support,* and *problem* questions.

- Who must do what? To whom, for whom, and with whom? Where and when and how?

- What resources will I need, and what resources will others need? Who must do what . . . to obtain them.

- What support will I need, and what support will others need? Who must do what . . . to obtain it?

- What problems will I encounter, and what problems will others encounter? Who must do what . . . to obtain what resources . . . to obtain what support . . . to solve those problems?

We explore each of the four groups of questions below, to enable you to discuss them and answer them in detail.

ACTION QUESTIONS

> *Who must do what? To whom, for whom, and with whom? Where and when and how?*

Answers to the action questions are typically stated simply and directly. For example, here's a goal set by a project manager, followed by the beginning of her plan to achieve it. She first describes a *task,* a major unit of work; then she describes the *action steps* necessary to complete the task. She uses imperatives to state the goal and the task. She uses complete sentences to describe the action steps, naming the person or department responsible for taking them.

> *Goal:* Put model into full production of 1,000 units per month by November 30.
> *Task 1:* Obtain raw materials by March 31.
> *Action Steps:*
> a. Project Manager (PM) and Project Engineer (PE) approve purchase orders and deliver to Purchasing Director (PD) by January 15.
> b. Purchasing obtains bids by ———PM and PE study bids with PD, and select contractors and suppliers by ———.
> c. PD places orders by ——— for delivery by ——— PE inspects materials by ——— and accepts delivery by ———.

Before discussing and determining *Who must do what?* (etc.), you may want to address the following preliminary questions to ensure you know who all the key players are:

- Who is going to take what kind of direct responsibility for working your plan or contributing to its success?

- Who can exercise what kind of direct formal authority to help you or hurt you?

- Who can exercise what kind of power over resources you need but don't control?

- Who has what kind of stake in what you're going to be doing and in knowing how it's going?

- Who has what kind of influence that can be used for good or for ill?

Your key players may include people whose advice and consent you'll need though they don't have direct authority over what you do or direct responsibility for your performance. For example, your key players may include people whose performance you'll affect by what you do and when you do it. If so, you may want to name them in your plans and give them constructive roles.*

RESOURCE QUESTIONS

What resources will I need, and what resources will others need? Who must do what . . . to obtain them?

Answering resource questions means asking yourself, *How much* and *how many* of *what kind* of resource? For example:

---

*Our *Who?* questions reflect ideas presented in *Influence Management* (Forum 1982), a seminar offered by the Forum Corporation for people who have to make and carry out plans when lacking formal authority over key players. For further information, please see our bibliography.

- How much of what kind of *time,* including productive time, calendar time, and elapsed time?

- How much of what kind of *plant, equipment, materials,* and *services?*

- How much *money* to cover what kind of costs, including direct and indirect costs, variable and fixed costs?

- How many of what kind of *people,* to do what jobs, and with how much of what kind of *knowledge, skill,* and *experience* to do them well?

The answers to these questions will often show that you've set goals and made plans that depend on obtaining scarce resources or resources that you cannot get. Common among them are the time to do all the things that you and others must do, including time to fix things that go wrong.

SUPPORT QUESTIONS

What support will I need, and what support will others need? Who must do what . . . to obtain it?

By *support* we mean voluntary assistance. You get it by asking for it and you get it from people who don't have to give it to you unless they want to. Ask yourself the following:

- Whose support are we *depending on?* Why them? Where and when? To perform what tasks and take what action steps?

- What tasks do we need support for? How much of what kind of support? From whom? Why them? Where and when? To take what steps?

- Whose support or what support do we need *so badly* that we ought to make getting it one of our major tasks?

- How much of what kind of support? From whom? Why them? Where and when? To do what?

You may want to revisit the support questions after discussing the problem questions below.

PROBLEM QUESTIONS

What problems will I encounter, and what problems will others encounter? Who must do what . . . to obtain what resources . . . to obtain what support . . . to solve those problems?

First ask yourself about **predictable** problems:

- What problems do we expect . . . in *achieving results?* In *obtaining resources?* In *securing support?*

- What should we do to *prevent* these problems from arising? To *correct* these problems if they do arise?

- What should we do if we can't prevent or correct *minor* predictable problems? *Major* predictable problems?

Next ask yourself about **contingencies,** focusing first on the problem of not being prepared for **bad** things to happen.

- What problems might arise unexpectedly that we'd *have* to solve? When? Why?

- Which would cost us dearly to solve? How much? Why?

- Which would cost us so dearly that we might have to *change* or *abandon* our goals?

- How should we *prepare* for facing such problems?

- How should we *lower the probability* of such problems occurring?

Now focus on the problem of not being prepared for **good** things to happen:

- What opportunities might arise unexpectedly that we'd *have* to seize? When and why might they arise?

- What opportunities might arise to *exceed* our goals or achieve them *at far less cost?*

- What opportunities might arise to set *higher* goals or *different* goals or *additional* goals?

- How should we *prepare* for seizing such opportunities?

- How should we *raise the probability* of such opportunities occurring?

Obviously, you can't predict what form good fortune might take, but you can envision events that would favor you unexpectedly. For example:

- You're achieving far better results than you expected, or achieving the results you wanted, but far more easily and quickly.
  - (*a*) What results? When? Why?
  - (*b*) In this event, what would you have the opportunity to do?

- You're obtaining far greater resources than you expected, or obtaining the resources you wanted, but far more easily and quickly.
  - (*a*) What resources? When? Why?
  - (*b*) In this event, what would you have the opportunity to do?

- You're getting far greater support than you expected, or getting the support you wanted, but far more easily and quickly.
  - (*a*) What support? When? Why?
  - (*b*) In this event, what would you have the opportunity to do?

After discussing the questions above, you can plan to make your own breaks.

EVALUATING PLANS

Before you try to achieve a goal and implement a plan, you need to conduct a cost-benefit analysis. You need to consider *all* the costs and benefits that are likely to result from an enterprise, not simply those intended and expected by its leaders and described in their goals and plans. You also need to consider *all* the people the enterprise is likely to affect, not simply those leaders and the people they intend to serve. Then you determine who is likely to bear what kind and degree of cost and who is likely to enjoy what kind and degree of benefit.

Then you can make an overall evaluation, considering the *expected rewards* for success and *expected penalties* for failure.

Costs

Plans typically identify the intended costs of an enterprise by answering the question, *How much and how many of what kind of resource do we need?* For example:

- How much of what kind of *time,* including productive time, calendar time, and elapsed time?

- How much of what kind of *plant, equipment, materials,* and *services?*

- How much *money* to cover what kind of costs, including direct and indirect costs, variable and fixed costs?

- How many of what kind of *people,* to do what jobs, and with how much of what kind of *knowledge, skill,* and *experience* to do them well?

When conducting a cost-benefit analysis, you consider the announced resource costs of the enterprise. You also consider its unintended or unstated costs, including its opportunity costs, social costs, political costs, and personal costs.

OPPORTUNITY COSTS

Opportunity costs are the costs of making a choice. For example, suppose you have opportunities to rent or buy. The opportunity cost of choosing to seek the benefits of renting is the opportunity to seek the benefits of buying. Here are questions to consider:

- What promising *alternatives* do we have for investing the resources required by our enterprise?

- How much of what kind of *value* do they offer us the opportunity to create?

- How much of what kind of *cost* would result from taking that opportunity?

SOCIAL COSTS

Social costs differ from operating costs. An operating cost is a cost incurred by an enterprise for the purpose of doing business. Typical operating costs include costs for people, plant, materials, and services. By contrast, a *social cost* is a cost that results from the operation of an enterprise, a cost *imposed* on a society or a community by an enterprise operating in it. Air and water pollution are typical social costs. Here are questions to consider:

- Will our enterprise result in significant social costs to others?

- Who will bear how much or how many of these social costs? When and where will people bear them?

- How much would it cost us to eliminate those social costs or to compensate others for them?

- Could we *ethically* pursue our enterprise if we didn't eliminate those social costs or compensate those people?

POLITICAL COSTS

Political costs result from making enemies, losing friends, acquiring a bad reputation, or impairing your ability to work effectively with others, as might happen, for instance, if you gave people reason to distrust you or regard you as unreliable. If your enterprise involves responding to a crisis or making difficult choices or doing something unpopular or doing something that people don't understand, then you can incur political costs no matter how fine a person you are and how worthy your enterprise is. Consider the questions that follow:

- What will we be doing that could make enemies for us or cost us friends, hurting us now and in the future?

- Whose support could we lose? For what? When and where? How and why?

- How great a political cost could we incur, as measured by the opportunities that others may close to us?

PERSONAL COSTS

Personal costs include the physical and emotional costs of anxiety, overwork, heavy travel, fear of failure, conflict with others, and damage to relationships with families and friends. They also include opportunity costs and political costs analogous to those described above.

Social and personal costs always include the costs of doing what's ethically and morally wrong.

Benefits

Just as the overall costs of an enterprise include its unintended and unstated costs, so the overall value created by it includes its unintended and unstated benefits.

OPPORTUNITY BENEFITS

The *opportunity benefits* of an enterprise are the opportunities the enterprise will enable you to take, including, for example, the opportunity to advance your career, or enter a new market, or conduct significant research.

Consider these questions:

- What promising opportunities could we have if we go ahead with this enterprise? When and where would the opportunities arise?

- How much of what kind of *value* could we have the opportunity to create? When, where, and how would we have the opportunity?

- How much of what kind of *cost* could result from taking that opportunity? When and where would the cost arise?

SOCIAL BENEFITS

Social benefits result when an enterprise already *providing* value *contributes* added value to a community without charging for it, such as when social and economic stability results from the operation of a neighborhood bank. Here are questions to consider:

- What can our enterprise do for our community without increasing our operating costs?

- Who will enjoy how much or how many of these social benefits? When and where will people enjoy these benefits?

- How do we have to conduct our enterprise to create this added value?

POLITICAL BENEFITS

Political benefits result from making new friends and connections, converting enemies into friends, acquiring a good reputation, and enhancing your ability to work effectively with others, such as might happen if you gave people reason to trust you or regard you as reliable. Here are questions to consider:

- What will we be doing that could make friends for us, helping us now and in the future?

- Whose support could we gain? For what? When and where? How and why?

- How great could our political benefits be, as measured by the opportunities that others may open to us?

PERSONAL BENEFITS

Personal benefits include such extrinsic rewards as praise, recognition, career advancement, and salary increases. They also include such key intrinsic rewards as personal development and the psychic income of success, the latter a rarely stated but always intended benefit for people who consistently perform to high standards and achieve their goals.

Social and personal benefits always include the benefits of doing what's ethically and morally right.

Expected Rewards and Penalties

Rewards include the benefits that you confer *by* achieving a goal and the benefits you receive *for* achieving a goal. *By* achieving your goal you create the value you intended to create. You also enable yourself to enjoy the experience of success. You may also confer additional social, political, and personal benefits on yourself and others. *For* achieving your goal, you may win a prize, get a raise, earn a promotion, or receive praise.

Penalties result from incurring unacceptable types or degrees of cost. For example, penalties result when you don't contain costs within reasonable limits, or when you fail to achieve results that justify your costs, or when you incur costs that are unacceptable in *any* amount or degree; *and* when you or others suffer pain or loss for incurring such costs. From a martinet you may suffer severely for overrunning your budget by 1 percent or by a single penny. From a pussycat or the Pentagon you may get a complaint for overrunning your budget by a distance measured in parsecs. For our purposes, the penalty is what counts, not the cost itself.

What justifies an enterprise is a favorable relationship between expected rewards and expected penalties, reflecting not only the consequences of success and the consequences of failure but also the probability of success and probability of failure.

Expected rewards and penalties are commonly compared by means of numerical aids to decision making called "weighting systems." Here's how to use such a weighting system.

First assign a percent probability to success and failure, for example, a 20 percent probability to a low probability of success and an 80 percent probability to a high probability of failure. Then assign a rating from 1 to 100 to the consequences of success and failure, for example, 80 for major potential rewards and 20 for minor potential penalties. Then multiply the probabilities by the consequences, yielding an index value for *expected rewards* and an index value for *expected penalties* (see below). Then compare the index values, asking whether you ought to commit to gaining the expected rewards at the risk of incurring the expected penalties.

In our first example, the expected rewards for success and expected penalties for failure receive the same index value.

	Success	Failure
Probabilities	20%	80%
Consequences	80	20
Index Values	16 (0.2 × 80)	16 (0.8 × 20)

Should you commit to such an enterprise? That depends on how you interpret the numbers. Some people might say you should go ahead with the enterprise, arguing that rewards are major, penalties are minor, and expected penalties are low. But other people might say you shouldn't, saying the expected rewards of success are low because the probability of success is low; moreover, the expected rewards are *too* low, compared to the expected penalties.

The nays would certainly prevail if the potential penalties were moderate rather than minor, for then the expected rewards would compare very unfavorably with the expected penalties:

	Success	Failure
Probabilities	20%	80%
Consequences	80	40
Index Values	16	32

If you still wanted to pursue the enterprise, the analysis might suggest that you ought to change your goal or your plans or both, thus modifying the variables. Suppose you could increase the probability of success without decreasing the potential rewards or increasing the potential penalties. The resulting change in index values would be dramatic. For example:

	Success	Failure
Probabilities	50%	50%
Consequences	80	40
Index Values	40	20

To change the variables, you can modify your goal, offering yourself the opportunity to pursue different but equally significant rewards at the risk of incurring different but no greater penalties. You can also adopt a better plan for pursuing the *same* goal at the risk of incurring the *same* penalties, but a plan that greatly reduces the probability of actually incurring those penalties.

Suppose you've set an elaborate goal to develop a new automobile engine. You could change the variables by eliminating an especially costly performance capability, thus reducing potential penalties to a far greater extent than potential rewards. Your new variables and values might look like this:

	Success	Failure
Probabilities	50%	50%
Consequences	60	20
Index Values	30	10

By eliminating that costly performance capability, you might also increase the probability of success significantly by releasing resources for other uses. Then your new variables and index values might look like this:

	Success	Failure
Probabilities	75%	25%
Consequences	60	20
Index Values	45	5

But **beware the bottom line.** It may not mean what it seems to say. Consider the following numbers:

	Success	Failure
Probabilities	99%	1%
Consequences	100	100
Index Values	99	1

An extreme case? No indeed. Let 100 represent the potential rewards of generating electric power so cheaply that we can give it away. Let 100 also represent the potential penalties of a meltdown. So great are the expected rewards of success that to many a mind the risk is well worth taking. But to many other minds, *no* risk is the only risk worth taking when the potential penalties of failure, no matter how unlikely, include a nuclear catastrophe.*

Assign and interpret the numbers with care. You're using them to help you compare factors that are inherently difficult to compare, such as cheap electricity and human lives. You're also using numbers to quantify your

---

*See Hayes (1989) for a discussion of three techniques for making decisions that involve "catastrophic consequences."

subjective sense of probabilities and consequences and to help you interpret what you sense—to give it form that helps you clarify your thinking. Bear in mind how you're likely to sense probabilities, whether optimistically or pessimistically or cautiously. Interpret realistically. Also bear in mind that you can easily overstate or understate the consequences, especially if you're trying to talk yourself into something or out of something, or to talk others into supporting you. Interpret *fairly*.

What you sense and then quantify, you next multiply. Consider the result as an interpretation modified by an interpretation—as a product which itself requires interpretation, not as the reliable product of a mathematical equation or a chemical formula.

CHAPTER 7

Identifying the Causes of Problems

DEFINITIONS

Asked to define what a problem is, a lot of people would simply say that a problem is *something we want to do something about.* No wonder nothing gets done, or that what gets done doesn't do anything good.

In this chapter, we're going to suggest four ways of discussing and analyzing problems informally, using terms we expect will help you define what you're talking about effectively so you can do something about it constructively.

Problem

A problem is a situation you want to change either because something bad is happening or because something good is not happening. To solve your problem, you first have to determine what's causing it. Then you can look at alternatives for changing the situation. Then you can set goals and make plans to change it.

Necessary Cause

When something bad is happening, you identify its *necessary causes,* that is, those conditions that have to be present for that bad situation to continue. Then you decide which of those necessary causes you want to remove. The bad situation can't continue unless all of its necessary causes continue to be present; therefore, to change the bad situation, you don't have to remove *all* of its necessary causes; rather, you only have to remove *one* of them. For example, to put out a fire, you can pour water on the substance that's burning, bringing its temperature down below the point of ignition, or you can cover the burning substance with noncombustible substances to keep oxygen from reaching it.

Sufficient Cause

When something good is not happening, you identify its *sufficient cause,* that is, all of those conditions that have to be present collectively for a future situation that's good to replace the current situation that's not good. Right now, what's good isn't happening, because one or more of its necessary causes is absent. To make it happen, you must change the situation by introducing all its missing necessary causes, thus bringing into being its sufficient cause.

More precisely, you must change the situation by introducing the *specifically necessary* forms of all the missing *generically necessary* causes. For example, suppose you want to start a campfire. You've got a bright sun, dry wood, dry tinder, kitchen matches, and a magnifying glass. By education and experience, you've learned that three conditions are *generically* necessary for combustion: (1) oxygen must be present, (2) a combustible substance must be present, and (3), the temperature of that substance must have reached its point of ignition. You study your situation, looking for the *specifically* necessary conditions that apply. You've got the generically necessary oxygen freely available in its specifically necessary gaseous form. In dry wood and dry tinder you've got two specifically necessary forms of the generically necessary combustible substance. What you're missing is the specifically necessary temperature to ignite the tinder. To introduce that missing condition, you can use your matches or your magnifying glass. Probably you'll use your magnifying glass so you can save your matches to start an evening campfire.

We use the term *generically necessary cause* to describe a set of necessary conditions potentially containing an infinite variety of *specifically necessary causes* that can differ widely in kind and degree from one situation to the next. For example, *motive* can be called a generically necessary cause of human behavior that includes but isn't limited to *money,* for money is specifically necessary in some situations but not in others.

We use the term *specifically necessary cause* to describe the form a generically necessary cause must take in a particular situation. For example, if the situation involves a business transaction, then the generically necessary *motive* that must be present might take specifically necessary form as "$1 million U.S., payable by cashier's check no later than the coming 30th of June."

Means, Motive, and Opportunity

We regard *means, motive,* and *opportunity* as the generically necessary causes of human action and inaction. People *do* things in particular situations because those generically necessary causes are *present* in specifically necessary forms. And people *don't* do things because those generically necessary causes are *absent* in specifically necessary forms.

Where people are doing bad things, analyzing the problem means discovering what specifically necessary forms of means, motive, and opportunity are present, causing them to do those bad things. Solving the problem means removing whichever forms are most desirable and feasible to remove.

Where people aren't doing good things, analyzing the problem means discovering what specifically necessary forms of means, motive, and opportunity are absent, preventing them from doing those good things. Solving the problem means introducing all of the missing generically necessary causes, in whichever forms are most desirable and feasible to introduce.

Means can take the form of skills, knowledge, information, and experience, or of tools, technology, materials, and equipment. *Motive* can take the form of costs and benefits, of rewards and penalties, of emotional sense or rational sense. And *opportunity* can take the form of occasion to act or time to act or place to act, close by or far away, very often or rarely, for a day or for a year.

An analysis of means, motive, and opportunity enables you to determine how complex a situation is. For example, suppose you want people to cooperate in particular ways (that's *good*), but people aren't cooperating (that's *not good*). You pose three basic questions for discussion: What *means* for cooperating do people lack? What *motives* for cooperating do they lack? What *opportunities* for cooperating do they lack? Discussion might result in any or all of the following hypotheses or conclusions.

Means: People lack an efficient internal telephone system or an effective management information system. Or they lack the skills to confront conflict constructively or the skills to repair broken relationships.

Motives: People don't gain anything by cooperating or lose anything by not cooperating. Or they don't know what they stand to gain by cooperating or what they stand to lose by not cooperating. Or they lose by cooperating in the way we want them to cooperate, while they gain by doing something we don't want them to do, that is, by competing against each other destructively to curry favor with their bosses.*

Opportunities: People don't hold regular formal or informal meetings, or their bosses do all the talking at the meetings they do hold. Or people don't understand each other's needs because they hold very different types of jobs.

An analysis of means, motive, and opportunity may well demonstrate that you can't set a goal to *solve* a problem; rather, you must set a goal to *manage* it. For example, suppose you've called a meeting to discuss how to eliminate arson in your troubled city. People point out that *means* include rags, bottles, candles, matches, gasoline, newspapers, and magnifying glasses; that *motives* include pleasure, profit, anger, and greed—the pathologies of reason as well as those of emotion; that *opportunity* is ubiquitous, presenting itself wherever buildings made of combustible substances are found.

Clearly, you can't stop arson from occurring, because you can't remove *all* means or *all* motives or *all* opportunities for arson. The generically necessary causes are

---

*Cf. Robert F. Mager and Peter Pipe, *Analyzing Performance Problems,* Part III (Mager and Pipe 1970, pp. 47–90). Questions addressed include *Is desired performance punishing? Is non-performance rewarding? Does performing really matter?*

present in forms so numerous and varied that you cannot eliminate each and every one of them. But you can *manage* the problem by limiting it. For example, effective law enforcement can greatly reduce motive. And effective tenant and neighborhood organizations can greatly reduce opportunity by maintaining a close watch on dangerous property owners and endangered buildings.

Finally, as a brief case history will show, a thorough analysis of means, motive, and opportunity can help you avoid a common pitfall—that in solving a problem by making a quick fix you may be exchanging one bad situation for another.

Case History

A company's agricultural chemical production workers were found to be suffering exposure to a known teratogen, dioxin, a substance that causes birth defects. The substance was a by-product of an otherwise innocent manufacturing process. The company's production workers included men and women.

The existing situation was *bad*: women capable of bearing children were being exposed to the substance. The desired situation was *not bad*: women capable of bearing children would not be exposed to the substance.

An analysis of means, motive, and opportunity would have shown that specifically necessary causes of the bad situation included the following:

- *Means:* the materials and processes necessary for production of dioxin

- *Motive:* the workers' needs for well-paying jobs

- *Opportunity:* the job duties of the women and the working conditions that brought dioxin into contact with them.

But no analysis was made.

Ignoring *means* and *motive,* management chose to remove a specifically necessary *opportunity* for the problem to arise, that specifically necessary cause of the problem which was quickest, cheapest, and easiest to remove, namely, the women. They took the women off the production line, reassigning them to office jobs at lower wages.

No women, no problem.

Management said nothing about *means,* nothing about perhaps changing the manufacturing process to prevent the production of dioxin, thus removing a different specifically necessary cause of the problem, the teratogen itself. Management did not consider *motive,* such as offering the women incentives to exchange production jobs for other jobs. And management said nothing about changing working conditions on the production line that brought dioxin into contact with the women. In other words, they gave the women no reason to believe that they'd consider removing *opportunity* in any of its forms save that of the women themselves.

Several women underwent hysterectomies, then demanded to be reinstated.

No uterus, no problem.

FOUR INFORMAL METHODS OF ANALYZING PROBLEMS

We'll now present four common informal methods of analyzing problems to identify their generically necessary and specifically necessary causes. They include

- the Method of Analogy
- the Method of Simulation
- the Method of Comparison
- the Method of Relationships

By *informal methods* we mean methods that generally work well under conditions where rigid standards of proof don't have to be met; however, as you'll see, we don't mean methods that are sloppy.

The Method of Analogy

To use the Method of Analogy, you first decide that you're looking at a case of something you know about, for example, a situation that's *bad,* where people are shouting at each other angrily, or a situation that's *not good,* where people won't listen to each other. Then you draw on your knowledge and experience to develop a diagnostic model of cause and effect for those types of situations; in other words, you look for familiar patterns.

When the situation is bad, your model describes what's likely to be wrong generically and directs your attention to particular necessary conditions that are likely to be present. For example, when you're looking for ways to stop a shouting match, your model will probably tell you to look for instances of misunderstanding.

When the situation is not good, you use a different model that describes all the generically necessary causes of the outcome you want. This model directs your attention to particular necessary conditions that are likely to be absent. For example, when you're looking for ways to get people to listen to each other, your model might tell you to look for signs that people lack a common vocabulary and then determine what kind of vocabulary they need.

To use the Method of Analogy, you can pose three basic questions that necessarily call for recognition of familiar patterns:

- What's going on?
- What's going right?
- What's going wrong?

You can also pose questions that call explicitly for pattern recognition:

- What's *generally* likely to be going wrong in a situation like this?
- What's *actually* likely to be going wrong?
- What actually *is* going wrong?

When the situation is bad, you can ask people to describe what's typically present as *means, motive,* and *opportunity* in similar situations.

When the situation is not good, you can ask them what's typically absent in similar situations.

Periodically, you should also ask people to give examples of the type of experience on which they're basing their answers. Make sure they're applying valid models of causation reflecting knowledge of truly analogous situations, for when people apply the wrong diagnostic models they can solve the wrong problems, often with disastrous results. For example, knowing nothing of working conditions, they can treat the lung diseases of miners and textile workers solely as the product of conditions in the home and the neighborhood.

The Method of Simulation

Many problems are solved experimentally by a process of simulated trial and error. Briefly, you propose to remove particular conditions from situations that are bad and propose to introduce particular conditions into situations that are not good. Then you test for effect by simulation, asking what would happen if you actually removed or introduced those conditions. For example, you could pose the following questions about a situation in which morale was bad:

- What if we reduced the number of status reports that people have to file?

- What would change for the better? How much for the better?

- What would change for the worse? How much for the worse?

You could pose similar questions about a situation in which morale was not good:

- What if we added the option of writing a term paper instead of taking an exam?

- What would change for the better? How much for the better?

- What would change for the worse? How much for the worse?

The Method of Simulation appeals to people who want to solve problems quickly, want to make sure they solve them thoughtfully rather than going for a quick fix, and want to consider a variety of proposals for action so they can develop a thorough understanding of the causes of problems before they act.

The Method of Comparison

To use the Method of Comparison, you contrast situations that are bad with similar situations that are *not* bad and situations that are not good with similar situations that *are* good, looking for points of difference and ideas about what to do.

Typically, you pose three general questions:

- What happens and doesn't happen in happy situations where people have either solved our problem or have never had it?

- By contrast, what *is* or *isn't* happening in our unhappy situation?

- So what do we think *should* or *should not* be happening?

By comparing answers from one situation to another, people can develop a cause-and-effect model of their situation *as it should be* and an understanding of their situation *as it is*. They can then propose necessary causes to remove or necessary causes to introduce. For example, if a condition present in all happy situations is absent from all unhappy ones, then a reasonable person might conclude that the missing condition is a cause of the problem.

But risk of error remains. The sample of happy cases that people are considering may not be large enough to result in a complete model of the situation as it should be. And the happy cases selected for study may not be truly comparable to the unhappy case. For example, critical conditions for success in selling a product to department stores may differ significantly from critical conditions for success in selling that same product to supermarket chains; if so, cases of success with the two types of customer will not be comparable, nor will cases of failure.

The Method of Relationships

Using the Method of Relationships, you construct and compare a model of the situation *as it is* with a model of the situation *as it should be,* considering the one as a system producing your unsatisfactory *actual* results and the other as a system producing your *desired* results. Here are the steps you take:

1. Construct a model of the situation as it should be: Who *should* be doing what by when? Where and why and how? To whom, for whom, and with whom? And who should be doing what how well . . . to produce your desired results?

2. Construct a model of the situation as it is: Who *is* doing what by when? Where and why and how? To whom, for whom, and with whom? And who is doing what how well . . . to produce your actual results?

3. Compare the models in every respect:
   • Who, what, by when: desired and actual
   • Where, why, how . . .
   • To whom, for whom, with whom . . .
   • What, how well . . .

To construct your model of the situation as it should be, identify all major phases of the work required to achieve your desired results, then break down each phase into major tasks, then build a model for each of those tasks. To identify phases and tasks, determine at what points in the process a person responsible for *overall* results would want to evaluate *interim* results, because at those points, she or he will know whether

- a significant body of work has successfully been completed
- any significant problems have been encountered
- time remains to solve those problems without jeopardizing overall results

Problems frequently arise at those points where a first group of people is supposed to complete a significant body of work in such a way that a second group of people can begin another significant body of work, that is, at points where the performance of a first group becomes critical to the performance of a second. Describing such points, workers often speak of "leaves," managers of "handoffs," and consultants of "interfaces."

Often, no standards are set for completing one task in a way that contributes to successful performance of the next task. Management evaluates performance of the first against standards set for that task only, without regard for performance of the next task or the overall success of the enterprise. So people do things without regard for the needs of others. For example, they perform the task in whatever manner they like, thereby creating significant problems for others. Or people encounter a significant problem they should solve, and failing to solve it, they cover it up and pass it on.

CHAPTER 8

Announcing and Doing Groundwork for a Discussion

GIVING ADVANCE NOTICE: HOW AND HOW NOT TO DO IT

Some discussions simply don't require formal advance notice or an announced agenda. Whether they happen spontaneously or by design, the agenda is given in the request. For example, if a colleague approaches you and says, "Ann, could we discuss the Adnoidol nasal spray proposal to the Food and Drug Administration?" you wouldn't reply, "Oh yes, George, just as soon as you've worked out a date, time, and agenda." Rather, you would be more likely to reply, "Sure, George, now or later on?" The resulting discussion is no less a discussion for being informal. Indeed, in the circumstances, it is probably more of a discussion, with fewer hidden factors or motives, for being informal than if George had sent Ann a memorandum (or if she had demanded one) stating the date, time, place, and topic of their discussion. The latter sets off alarm bells, and signals a degree of "seriousness" that, if not intended, could easily interfere with a frank exchange of viewpoints and information.

On the other hand, other discussions, particularly those involving several persons or a large group, will require both advance notice and a list of topics to be discussed. Such formal notice might look like this:

CLINICAL MONITORS MEETING

Monday, 24 April
2:00–4:00 p.m.
Elliott Laboratory, Room 112

AGENDA

1. Minutes of the 5 March Clinical Monitors Meeting
2. Report on new guidelines from the Food and Drug Administration
3. Implications of the new guidelines for the Adnoidol nasal spray proposal to the FDA
4. Recommendations for further testing and rewrite of the Adnoidol proposal

Note that the announced agenda not only calls attention to new FDA guidelines but also calls for inquiry into their implications and for recommendations for more testing and also for a rewrite of the Adnoidol proposal. Had the latter items (3 and 4) been omitted from the announcement *but then brought up as main points,* confusion could well have resulted. For example, "I thought we were here to discuss the new guidelines in general, not the Adnoidol proposal!" "Rewrite the Adnoidol proposal? How do we know there's anything wrong with it as it stands?" Implications lead to recommendations, and by announcing them as items for discussion, you eliminate much of the extraneous "static" and defensiveness that is a natural response to being caught off guard.

In general, a written call for discussion should contain the following information:

- A list of the participants either by name or by collective reference, as in the example above

- The date, time, and place of the meeting

- A brief statement of the topic(s) to be discussed

- Some indication of the sequence of topics to be discussed, usually by numbering them in order

- Some indication of the results to be achieved, as in item 4 in the example above

Supporting documents or other information supplied in advance should be noted in parentheses under the relevant items. If there are time constraints or deadlines for making decisions, offering recommendations, or producing results, they too should be noted. Failure to do so could result in complaints at being rushed along, or worse, expressions of resentment at being "railroaded" by the chair.

ON HAVING A PURPOSE

As mentioned at the outset of this book, every discussion has a cognitive purpose. Failure to be clear about that purpose or to announce it in your agenda can short-circuit a group discussion quicker than water on a spark plug. Without a focus, you are left wide open to irrelevant intrusions and tangential meanderings. So how do you get clear on your purpose?

First off, *never* summon people to a discussion the purposes of which are unclear or hidden, if you can help it (cf. Frank 1989, pages 30–31). Unless you like confusion and provocation, the results are likely to be unproductive in the extreme. For example, if you call a meeting to discuss the future direction of the department with the secret intention of screening, or eliminating, candidates for head of the department, don't be surprised if others see through your ruse and create havoc. Dissembling is risky business unless you are a past master of the politics of meetings. But, after all, that isn't discussion, is it? Manipulation and discussion are categorical opposites, for discussion depends on respect, honesty, frankness, and objectivity.

Here are questions to ask yourself when your aim is understanding:

- What is the central issue at stake?

- What do people need to know to discuss that issue?

- What feelings and attitudes about that issue need to be taken into account?

- What do you want or expect people to do about that issue?

Keeping these four simple questions in mind as you plan a discussion and prepare an agenda will save you endless amounts of grief. You might also consider how you want people to feel about you at the end of the discussion. Were you an effective facilitator? Did you maintain a balanced outlook? Did you give ample opportunity to minority opinions? Did you encourage the reticent to speak up? Where you able to keep the talk on track? Were your summaries accurate? Were you *fair?*

SOME NOT-SO-SIMPLE MECHANICS

The preferred physical settings for a discussion are a round table or a circular or semicircular open-seating arrangement in which all the participants can face each other as well as the discussion leader. Other table arrangements include the familiar **U, V,** and **[}** shapes, with participants seated around the perimeters. Psychologically, these are the most "democratic" arrangements, allowing for easiest direct address among the participants. A variation on the round table is the boardroom arrangement: an oblong or rectangular table with the discussion leader situated at one end and the participants down the sides.

As a general rule, the longer and narrower the table, the greater the attention focused on the leader.

It is very difficult to promote an open discussion from a stage at a distance from the audience unless you are very practiced at that format. More likely, attention will focus entirely on you and your opinions, and discussion will be more on the order of question and answer with little interaction among audience members. That is the typical lecturer's format for which most classrooms were designed. Open discussion among participants is further hampered in such a setting by the fact that people are constrained to talk over their shoulders to those in the back of the room or into the backs of the heads of those in front of them.

Two rough generalizations may help guide you in your choice of venue and format.

First, *the larger the group, the more difficult the "staging" of discussion becomes.* Two or three people sitting together at a seminar table or in chairs in front of a television camera (as in William F. Buckley's *Firing Line*) is a relatively easy stage to set. The transition number is somewhere between fifteen and twenty participants; for then the group becomes a crowd, equal access among all individuals is reduced, and nonparticipation by some is increased. In the authors' experience, upwards to sixty people *can* be accommodated in a relatively open discussion (where participants talk to each other, not just to or through the leader) if something resembling the semicircular seating arrangement can be preserved—for example, in a classroom with movable chairs arranged in two tiers around the edges of the room. A curved ampitheater setting also promotes spontaneous interaction better than flat seating does. With such numbers, however, a measure of control beyond minimum guidance is required to hold course and stave off confusion.

Second, *the larger the group, the more the discussion leader's role becomes a controlling one.* A controlling role is a matter of choice in smaller groups, but it is a necessity for the management of larger groups. This means that the discussion leader frequently needs to exert his or her influence to keep things on track: asking questions, directing speakers to each other, selecting speakers from the floor, encouraging nonspeakers to participate, discouraging others who speak too much, indicating when discussion is wandering from the topic, setting time limits, and so on.

Doing groundwork for a discussion includes considering what use you want to make of mechanical and audiovisual aids such as overhead projectors, microphones, slide projectors, flipcharts, videotapes, chalkboards, and printed displays. We offer the following rules of thumb for the use of technology:

- Keep your use of audiovisual devices to a minimum so you can minimize the possibility of malfunction, and also be prepared to carry on without them.

- Consider using prepared supporting materials such as outlines, illustrations, diagrams, maps, equations, or transparencies where necessary to simplify communication and save time.

- Consider using flipcharts and chalkboards to record salient points and crucial questions, facts, and opinions as they arise *during* the discussion. (Flipcharts also help you record questions when many are coming from the floor at once.)

- Let *discussion* and not your attachment to a favorite slide, diagram, or video segment determine the direction of talk. Always be prepared for unanticipated developments and new turns of thought. Be prepared to sacrifice the media to the message.

ROUTINE AND NONROUTINE DISCUSSIONS

Doing groundwork for a discussion often means no more than preparing an agenda, providing supporting information and choosing a venue, provided the discussion is routine. For example, a collegial discussion among research scholars in a specialized field such as artificial intelligence usually requires little more than notice of the time, place, topic, and relevant documents (usually a paper in progress or some newly published development in the field); so also a routine business discussion of past results and current plans.

Other discussions do require special preparation, particularly those having to do with highly controversial or emotionally charged issues. For example, a prenatal class in natural childbirth for first-time parents is hardly a routine matter for the participants. People are nervous, expectant(!), confused, and don't know what to do or how to prepare for the class. They need reassurance and some psychological coaching in advance. Who should attend? Will a physician be there to give advice? What are the risks of natural childbirth? Can anyone opt for it? What is "unnatural" about other methods? These and many more questions will be dealt with in detail in the class; but the obvious ones that leap to mind may be "previewed" in an initial counseling session designed to allay fears and inform participants of what to expect.

Similarly, a discussion of applicants' credentials for tenure in an academic department, however routine in one sense (i.e., recurrent, standard procedure), is very special in another. Namely, peoples' careers and security are at stake; major decisions affecting those people have to be made. The future configuration of the department will also be affected. Such meetings require careful preparation, including stipulation of conditions of confidentiality, relevant and irrelevant factors (such as personality clashes), departmental priorities, budgetary limits, and the like.

Truly routine discussions may require advance information but do not require special preparation, psychologically or otherwise. Nonroutine discussions require both advance information and one or more forms of special preparations, generally involving information, organization, physical arrangements and sensitivity to people's needs, concerns, strengths and weaknesses. Here are two case studies.

Case 1

You have been elected chair of the Committee on South African Educational Exchanges for your university, community college, or school board. The question has arisen, what can your institution do to promote faculty and student exchanges, in particular to assist black South African students to attend your institution? A member of the African National Congress (ANC), currently on a lecture tour, has agreed to attend a meeting to discuss the matter. Aside from announcing the date, time, and place of the meeting and the subject of discussion, what special preparations should you make?

First, get more *information*. Who and what are the students and institutions in question? Are their levels of study and preparation comparable to those of your institution? Who will foot the bills and how? Are there any among your faculty who would like to teach there? Conversely, who among their faculty would like to teach at your institution? Again, who will foot the bills? How can such an exchange be arranged? Who is the ANC representative? What is his background? Is he qualified to speak for others, make decisions, recommendations? Obviously, prior to the meeting, you cannot have answers to all these questions—at least, not in detail—*but you should be looking for the answers to such questions and considering their implications.*

As for *organization,* prudence and politics would suggest that the ANC visitor be given every opportunity to express his views, answer questions, and make suggestions. (You won't have another go at him, so make the most of it.) Participants should be alerted, formally or informally, to the unique opportunity to garner information and suggestions from an authoritative source. You may also want to suggest that participants focus on policy questions rather then questions of administrative detail such as class schedules, specific course requirements, budgetary allocations, and the like, which can afford to be set aside. You don't want a foreign visitor to get bogged down in such relatively trivial matters.

Sensitivity will be required to get the most out of the

ANC representative. He won't be back, so how to make him feel comfortable? What can you do to make him feel welcome, draw him out? What are your own peoples' concerns in hosting him? Are they enthusiastic, reluctant, suspicious? Be sure to ask. Are you prepared to turn the meeting over to him if he displays a strong personality and sense of direction? Think about the advisability of that: it may or may not be a good idea.

Questions to be asked about *physical* arrangements include the following: What audiovisual equipment does the ANC representative need? Where would he feel most comfortable sitting? Next to you as chair? Among the other participants? Will he need a microphone? Will other South African representatives be present? What then should the seating arrangements be? Be frank and ask. Your guest will be grateful and your committee will be set at ease. The result will be a far more profitable and edifying discussion. All these matters are your responsibility as chair, and you cannot lose by attending to them.

Case 2

You have just been appointed to chair the conservation commission of a large and complex urban center. The commission is a volunteer organization consisting of a full-time administrative director and part-time volunteers: doctors, engineers, academics, lawyers—all busy with their own jobs. The commission screens developers' applications, approving or disapproving them, with a primary mandate to protect the wetlands and manage flood control in the vicinity of a river that flows through the town. What can you do to assure that discussion of a given application is both thorough and fair?

You have a special problem with prior information that directly affects the organization of the discussion. The problem is a classic double bind: the relevant information is highly technical and voluminous, yet the commission members, though expert in their separate domains, are volunteers and cannot be expected to come to the meeting fully informed. Some will try, but much time will have to be spent bringing members up to speed on the facts and figures of the case in question. *This means you must plan to allow them to inform themselves during the discussion by asking and answering technical questions, querying the documents, and hashing through other details.*

This situation contrasts with discussions in business, academic, or other professional settings, in which participants can be expected to come prepared on the basic facts and issues as presented in the advance material. Not so in volunteer organizations, where much of the informing occurs in the course of discussion. That in turn requires your special patience as discussion leader, particularly if you are accustomed to peer discussions among professionals. Here the full-time administrative director can be of great assistance in sorting documents and directing people of relevant expertise to the vital passages. In effect, the administrative director should function as coleader of the discussion in a primarily informative capacity. For example, the engineer in the group, having been supplied with the relevant plans, suddenly notices a major flaw in the flood-control details of the sewage system for a new hotel complex. "Can the flaw be corrected?" you ask, or, consulting the lawyer, "Do we have legal grounds for disapproval?" "I'll have to think about that," both reply. And so it goes in relatively slow motion. But take solace from this: both questions *have* been broached and will now get the attention due them. In general, then, volunteer organizations require more time and assistance to mull things over and reach decisions, provision for which needs to be made when planning and organizing their discussions.

Being sensitive to participants' special concerns, the administrative director plays a vital role in making sure that the right information gets to the right people before and during the discussion. Legal, engineering, environmental, and aesthetic issues all come into play; and it is the administrative director's responsibility to sort documents and information relative to those issues. Your role is to draw out the expertise present in the group. That means having the sensitivity to determine what specific contributions of knowledge or judgment individual members of the commission can provide and the sensitivity to plan for addressing those members directly when an issue within their domain is going to come up. For example, if there is more than one lawyer or engineer on the commission, plan to get *them* into a discussion of legal implications. "Mary, we've heard George's legal opinion, what's yours?" "Larry, as a builder, do you think the sewer plans can be revised to comply with the law? Alice apparently thinks not, or is at least hesitant. Am I right, Alice?" In such a group, your responsibility is to keep the different balls rolling in the right directions; and that means knowing what they are and to whom they should be directed.

Special preparation for volunteer group discussions includes readying duplicate materials for review by people who didn't review the materials distributed prior to the meeting. Notepads should also be made available so people can record their major points for later collection by the chair and the administrative director. A tape recorder will relieve you and others of the need to take extensive notes.

MORE ON THE INFORMATION GIVEN

Having given people the advance information they need, what attitude should you adopt at the meeting when they don't do their homework? We suggest the following. *Assume that a minority of participants have actually read the advance material, but speak as if everyone had done so.*

Above all, don't make anyone feel stupid or delinquent in raising points of information or naive questions. Simply explain that this or that point is covered in the previously distributed document on pages thus and so. In effect, plan to take the high road by reviewing the agenda and purpose of the discussion and making sure that no one can *legitimately* ask, "What the hell is going on here?" People who have done their homework will thereby become your allies, taking up the issues as they should be addressed, and deflecting irrelevant or disruptive questions.

Having done your own homework, you may be understandably irritated at those who have not done the same; *but never show your irritation.* If you do, you will make people defensive and competitive rather than open and cooperative.

WHEN NOT TO CALL FOR A DISCUSSION

Before you call for a discussion, consider whether you are likely to encounter any of the five following conditions that cripple rational inquiry.

One-Way Conversation

When people talk *at* each other rather than to or *with* each other, that's one-way conversation. Discussions of such heated issues as acid rain, abortion, or euthanasia, not to mention many political debates, degenerate into one-way conversations if not into shouting matches. How many times have you heard someone in such a situation say, "Well, perhaps you are right on that point: I think you've changed my mind." Quite the contrary. The general attitude is exactly opposite to the spirit of inquiry: "I know what I think, believe what I believe, and nothing anyone says could change my mind." All sides are deaf to all other sides, and people consider it a *virtue* to be inflexible and adamant in their beliefs. By contrast, to take such an arrogant stand in a genuine rational discussion is one of the more common ways to short-circuit the inquiry.

Premature Closure

Rational discussion suffers from premature closure when someone has an urgent and often *hidden* agenda that calls for reaching a predetermined conclusion. Participants appear to be free to reach their own conclusions, but in fact they are not; rather, they're being subjected to manipulation.

Having an open agenda and leading people on to predetermined conclusions are not the same. An open agenda is a list of topics *to be discussed,* not a set of conclusions to be reached. If you already knew the conclusions, you wouldn't bother to discuss the topics. Admittedly, there are situations, particularly in education, where a good deal of "leading on" is necessary. And there is nothing wrong with closure as such; but *premature* closure is quite another matter.

Premature closure occurs when someone, usually the leader, limits discussion to points that he or she considers relevant, disallowing all others that could be relevant to the topic under discussion. Many teachers, especially those who follow a strict lesson plan or syllabus to the letter, are liable to close their ears to what they hear as "sidetracks" that head people away from their objectives. In true rational discussion, leaders establish through the inquiry whether a point is relevant, not rule it out of order arbitrarily.

Premature closure has a damping effect on exploration and discovery. You feel locked in on a hidden target. It's more important to "get the answer" than to explore the question.

Mutual Catharsis

Mutual catharsis is the opposite of premature closure. A spirit of "anything goes" prevails. Just about anything you want to say is relevant. The emphasis is less on what you *think* than on how you *feel*. For example, "How do you feel about that, Robert? Mary? Yeah, me too. I remember once . . ." The idea is to share "experiences," to listen for resonances within your own experience, perhaps just to bring them out. Many casual conversations are mutually cathartic and serve useful emotional purposes; but they don't represent rational discussion. Where the purpose of talking is to release and share feelings, it would be distinctly inappropriate to focus in on a thesis, topic, opinion, or belief with the purpose of analysis or reaching some conclusion. Better to avoid too much "discussion" at those times when expressing emotion is the point of talking. It's the skeptic, not the lover, who replies to "I love you" by asking, "Oh? How do you know?" This is not to say that shared (or unshared) feelings and experiences cannot be taken as data for discussion; but that is another level of talk altogether, one in which we all engage spontaneously, and therapists deliberately.

The Zero-Sum Game-Playing

In a zero-sum game, the contestants play "I win, you lose." When people approach discussion as a zero-sum game, they try to "*win* the argument" rather than *use* argumentation as a *means* to gain wisdom and act wisely. In short, they convert discussion into debate. This is a step up from one-way conversation, for both sides do listen to each other very carefully. But they do so only with the aim of finding an "opening," a flaw in the opponent's argument, which can be exploited to one's own advantage. Primary stress is upon *who* is right, not *what* is right. Political debates are typical of this sort of confrontation, in which to make a mistake is to lose points. Shortcomings and doubts about one's own opinions are scrupulously ignored while those of the opposition are relentlessly pursued. Openness is a weakness and changing one's mind a concession of defeat. Nothing better illustrates the essential difference between that view of discussion that sees it as part of "the scramble to win" and the "classical" view, espoused herein, of discussion as serving the interests of inquiry and understanding.

Social Correctness

Social correctness can block rational discussion by limiting what people can say, approvingly or disapprovingly, and also by requiring them to say something to be nice—and to be nasty. For example, if people dependent on the tobacco industry are engaged in a "discussion" of the medical effects of cigarette smoking, it's fairly certain that social pressures will favor the expression of some opinions over others, whatever the merits of the case. By the same token, a "discussion" of abortion by strongly partisan groups is more likely to end in confrontation than edification. It's not impossible for a reasonable dialogue to occur, but social pressures make the chances slim when positions are solidified. For then you must stand by your fellow combatants.

Social correctness also operates through conventions of deference: Who defers to whom? And why? So it is always apposite to ask, Under whose auspices is a "discussion" to be held? Is a change of mind or heart a real possibility? Or will the social conventions of deference not permit it? When your dean or division manager invites you in to "discuss" your promotion, you can be assured that negotiation is more the order of the day. On the other hand, when a teacher, colleague, or fellow researcher invites you to discuss a topic, then the objective is more likely to be knowledge than leverage.

Some corporations and institutions thrive on controversy and open discussion of issues; others do not. What kind of organization are you working in? Think about it. Authority, pecking order, or received opinion can greatly limit the possibilities of genuine discussion. Even more subtle are the cultural restraints on discussion. In some cultures, for instance, a junior person never speaks before, in front of, or in contradiction to, a senior person. Similarly, in some corporations—or educational institutions, for that matter—a lower-echelon person never contradicts an upper-echelon person. Such facts of life will usually be denied by those in control, but anyone who blunders into such constraints unaware soon learns their limits of tolerance.

The unhappy fact is that rational discussion is a rare and valuable social commodity, something to be cherished and cultivated at every turn for the sake not only of understanding, but of survival. To call for a discussion is to call for whatever truth unfettered reason can divine. Not everybody or organization can tolerate that threat.

CHAPTER 9

Behaving Thoughtfully: The Do's and Don'ts

Your basic obligation as leader is to *guide* discussion by asking questions, by listening and responding to others, and, as appropriate, by summarizing what has been said. (See Chapter Three.) In addition, if you choose a leadership role that allows or requires you to join the discussion, then you must also address key issues personally and oppose and support the views of other participants. And whatever the nature of your role, you must always bring discussion to an end.

In this chapter, we present numerous recommendations for performing those tasks with courtesy and respect, that is, for *behaving thoughtfully,* employing the social conventions of civility to help people do good thinking together. By observing those conventions you enable people to establish and preserve *face,* that is, to maintain their dignity and autonomy without having to defend themselves against attacks on their honor, competence, and character.* You do not make insulting statements like: "George, that's the silliest, stupidest remark that anyone's made all day. You must be crazy!" You also do not make imperious statements, for example, "George, your account of that matter has serious flaws to it. And I'll tell you what they are." Instead, you express disagreement civilly, saying, "George, *to my way of thinking,* your account of the matter *appears* to have some serious flaws to it. *Could I* tell you what *I think* they are?"

Using socially conventional phrases and sentence structures, like those highlighted above, enables you to honor the values of rational discussion—*respect* and *honesty,* and *frankness* and *objectivity.* In becoming an adult, you've learned how to use many such phrases and structures effectively, perhaps so effectively that you've forgotten you're applying social skills that you've had to learn. Hearing the blunt speech of a small child may remind you gently of all that you've learned. We offer the following recommendations, hoping we can help you continue to learn.

ASKING QUESTIONS AND SUMMARIZING

You ask questions to introduce a subject, to elicit information or opinions, to stimulate thinking, to arouse interest, to test for agreement or arrive at a conclusion, or simply to change the subject.

So, how to begin? A tried-and-true opening gambit is the *topical question* directing the participants to the subject you want them to address. You may start by establishing why the subject is of interest and importance. For example, suppose you are a teacher called upon to

---

*For a detailed treatment of "face" in social interaction, see *Politeness: Some Universals in Language Usage* (Brown and Levinson 1987).

lead a discussion on "critical thinking" with colleagues. Here's how you might start:

> Everybody says we need to teach students how to think more effectively. But they don't tell us what they mean; indeed, they probably don't know what they mean. As teachers, however, we do have to know what *we* mean. Otherwise, we can justly be accused of not knowing what we are doing.
>
> Two major questions face us:
> 1. What do we mean by *thinking?*
> 2. What do we mean by *effectively?*
>
> To begin, allow me to narrow the first major question: Does *thinking* include *feeling?* Or is *thinking* all cognition and no emotion?

At this point the topic is launched, and people are ready to pitch in. Don't be afraid to endure a few moments of silence while participants gather their thoughts. And if the silence becomes too leaden, don't be afraid to nudge someone gently. "John, you had some ideas on critical thinking over coffee yesterday. Would you mind sharing them to get us started?" If John prefers not to speak up just then, *be sure not to show irritation or displeasure* but quickly move on to another person—"Marie?" Use your common sense by calling first upon people who are, or appear to be, willing talkers. You may even ask one or two of the participants beforehand if they would be willing to kick things off. Such prior consultation takes you off the hook and shows that you value their opinions—saving your face and enhancing theirs.

As the discussion proceeds, think ahead to follow up questions by anticipating the direction that discussion will take. Typically, the discussion will follow the pro-con pattern earlier described: on the one hand *this,* on the other hand *that*. Certainly, you can expect someone to argue that thinking is a kind of problem-solving or computational skill, while someone else will counter with the claim that thinking in the broader sense is emotive. Once those, or similar, hypotheses are on the table, you are then in a position to raise a follow-up question: "Are there, then, different kinds of thinking, appropriate, perhaps, to different domains of learning and skill?" And so on, trying as best you can to keep the ball rolling in a polite, orderly fashion.

If you or anyone else wishes to raise a question of *meaning* regarding a vital term or statement, don't hesitate to raise it or let it be raised. "What do you mean by that?" is, in effect, a quest for common ground to avoid talking at cross-purposes. Indeed, it is one of your responsibilities as discussion leader to establish common ground so that the discussion can proceed profitably. Establishing a common terminology is crucial to finding common ground. Besides asking people to clarify their terms, another way of doing that is to ask for an illustration or example. "Could you give us an example, John, of what you mean by critical versus emotive thinking?" Then, pass the ball to someone else: "Marie, do you agree with the dichotomy that John has set up?" Note, the focus is less on the individuals talking than on what they say, on their statements, their assumptions, their reasons, arguments, definitions, evidence—*not their motives, characters, or personalities.*

Summarize periodically as appropriate. For example: "Correct me, please, if I misrepresent anyone's views, but it seems to me that the major positions taken thus far amount to this . . ." State your summary as briefly as possible; then let others step in and amend or correct it. This helps you to keep organized and draws the group towards, if not consensus, at least synopsis, a coherent

overview of the ground covered. Don't take all the responsibility upon yourself. Ask others to help summarize their opinions and positions earlier taken. That way,
no one can later say, "Well, my opinion [or evidence,
argument, distinction] just wasn't taken into account."
A delicate dynamic is now in place, the sustaining of
which depends as much on what you *don't* say as on what
you *do* say—that is, on how well you listen and respond.

LISTENING AND RESPONDING

To listen and respond effectively, listen not only for
the content of what is said, but also for the tone with
which it is said and for the emotional effect that it has.
Then make an *explicit* effort to let people know that you
want to understand them, grasp their meanings, value
their opinions, take them seriously. "Peter, could you
run that through again? I didn't quite grasp the last part."
Or, "Is it clear to everyone what Peter is getting at here?"

Also be sensitive to people as political and emotional
beings. For example, consider the following exchange.
John says, "Well, when it comes to thinking, in my experience women tend to focus on their feelings rather
than asking what can be done to change a situation."
Marie, a teacher of mathematics, replies, "John, I find
that insulting and sexist. Women can think critically and
rationally quite as well as men." *Don't intervene now. Let
the confrontation go on for a short while longer to allow for
face-saving qualifications.* John: "Well, what I mean is that
women seem to want more to ventilate their emotions
than to settle an issue." Marie: "Even in science or art?
Was Madame Curie merely ventilating her emotions in
her laboratory discussions? Are Iris Murdoch's psychological novels mere emotional outpourings?" *Now is the
time to step in to avoid a heated digression that could short-*

circuit the whole discussion. You: "The question before us is, What is effective thinking? [In other words, reassert the agenda as announced.] Now, if there are sex differences as regards critical thinking, what are they? What is the evidence for them? Are they greater or less than other differences, say, of intelligence or social class? And finally, what bearing, if any, do they have on the teaching of thinking skills in particular disciplines?"

In this way, *by asserting the agenda, not your opinion,* you insult no one, ignore no one, take no side, but you do succeed in bringing the focus back to the original issue while putting the onus on the participants to show how their opinions and differences bear upon the central question before the group.

General Guidelines

By observing the following general guidelines you can greatly help people establish and maintain face while preventing them from losing face.

1. *Reduce risk* by creating a climate in which people can make controversial or provocative statements with reasonable safety, and can test their ideas and tentative thoughts in ways that allow them to concentrate on expressing themselves and hearing others, not on protecting themselves politically or emotionally.

Reducing risk means reducing the fear of making mistakes. The ability to learn from mistakes is fundamental to collective inquiry, for mistakes, as we've previously said, are important *experimental results.* To generate those results means encouraging people to experiment without fear that they'll get the "wrong" answer.

2. As we'll reiterate later, a key way to reduce risk is to *avoid responding judgmentally to others.*

3. In addition, you should also *give people the benefit of the doubt,* treat them *objectively* as rational people, though they may not appear to be making any sense. Given their *assumptions,* what these people are saying might actually make very good sense. You will want to surface their assumptions to see what bearing they may have on the matter at hand, or to help the people ground themselves more firmly in reality. "Mary, that's an interesting way of looking at things. How would you argue for it?" People who see they can trust you with their conclusions may be willing to trust you with the assumptions that underlie them.

4. Also, as we'll reiterate later, another key way to reduce risk is to *welcome and accept appropriate statements of emotional and political concern.*

5. By *welcoming and accepting people unconditionally* you can help them free themselves of unreasonable fears and suspicions, dispel unfounded anger and hostility, substitute reasonable caution, and concentrate on the dialogue of discovery.

Specific Guidelines for Listening Effectively
Here are specific guidelines for listening and responding effectively.

- *Listen attentively* without interrupting, guarding against impatience or irritation. Look at whoever is speaking as if you were hanging on his or her every word, which, in fact, will enable you to do so.

- *Listen empathetically,* if not sympathetically, to the person who is speaking, to the personality, the emotions, the motives behind the statements made. In short, try to put yourself in the other person's shoes.

- *Listen constructively* to what is being said; that is, try to hear the strongest possible case that can be made for the position taken. By doing this, you will encourage people to develop and strengthen their arguments or to modify them.

- *Listen analytically* to relevant remarks, asides, examples, and particularly to terminology: to the pivotal concepts and ideas invoked to make a point or case. Remember the ground-clearing question, "What do you mean by . . . ?"

- *Listen retrospectively,* echoing to yourself in paraphrase what you hear. You might even take notes in your own words to the effect of "I think so and so is saying . . ." Such jottings become the basis for follow-up questions of the form, "Were you advocating . . . ?" "Do you mean to say . . . ?" "Are you seriously suggesting . . . ?"

- *Listen with an open mind,* especially where you disagree, making sure you hear what they are saying, not what you want or expect them to say. And do not close your mind in order to frame your next challenging question. Let that question come naturally, at the appropriate time, and not as a packaged response.

- *Listen with your eyes,* alert to signs of interest and enthusiasm, boredom or fatigue. Read the "signs" of body language, exchanged glances, tones of voice, facial expressions, noddings of agreement or disagreement, fidgeting impatience, discomfort, and the like. Discreetly watch other people and take note of their reactions to what is said.

Specific Guidelines for Responding Effectively

A *cardinal rule for leaders is never to respond judgmentally to others.* Instead, respond receptively, neither approving nor disapproving, in order to open your own mind and to build participants' trust in you. Show them that you want to understand all sides, not to win or dispute or condemn. The more controversial the topic and the more directive (as contrasted with participatory or collegial) the discussion leader's role, the more this cardinal rule applies. Here are some important ways of responding objectively to others rather than judgmentally.

- *Say nothing,* to give people time to think, to formulate their statements. Show them that you expect them to think for themselves. Don't succumb to the temptation to fill the silence with idle prattle or to lecture on the topic yourself.

- *Say as little as possible,* to get people talking. "John?" "Marie?" If asked to repeat the question, do so in as near identical terms as you can. Let them suggest any reformulations or tentative answers.

- *Play fair,* giving everyone who wants to respond the opportunity to do so without interruption. If certain individuals run on too long or hog the floor, gently suggest that there are others to be heard from. "Could we hear from someone who has not spoken?"

- *Play tough,* highlighting differences of opinion as sharply as possible and challenging participants to clarify their positions and supply supporting evidence or sources, as in the exchange between John and Marie above over sex differences in critical thinking. If someone makes a particularly offensive or egregious remark, silence is often *your* best response. Let the group make the first effort to bring the discussion back on track.

- *Acknowledge responses verbally,* by saying, "I see," by asking for amplification on certain points, by thanking those who spoke first for starting things off, by encouraging participants to speak up. "Well, it's clear where Fred stands on this subject. Anyone disagree?" or "Anyone care to add anything here?"

- *Clarify statements made, positions taken, and putative facts* by paraphrasing them and asking questions of meaning. "George, do I correctly understand you to be saying that . . . ?" "Joan, could you elaborate on your use of the term *critical* in your analysis of critical thinking?" Remember the all-important task of keeping people on common ground to prevent them talking past one another.

- *Acknowledge legitimate emotional or political concerns* where and when they arise, but keep the focus on exactly what is said, not the heat or vehemence with which it is said. Insist on rational treatment. "Marie, I recognize your strong feelings on this issue, but could we hear the evidence supporting your position?" Defusing anger and personal confrontation is one of your more delicate tasks. Be explicit: "People, could we please keep this on the plane of reason rather than the mountaintops of indignation?"

- *Reassert the agenda* whenever things seem to be getting out of hand or digressing from the central topic. The more controversial the topic, the more likely the discussion will take the form of emotional confrontation. The more technical the topic, the more likely the digression will take the form of an irrelevant tangent. Mind you, sidetracks can be immensely profitable and creative, but only you, in your capacity as leader, can decide when the central issue has been lost sight of.

ADDRESSING KEY ISSUES WHILE LEADING A DISCUSSION

Except when you are playing a purely moderating role, you will have opportunity to get involved in the discussion. That means wearing both hats: that of discussion leader and of participant. When and how should you present your own views? That's a judgment call. You'll probably prefer to wait until others have presented their views, so as not to focus undue attention on your own. But if you're in a position of authority, you may want to sketch your own views quickly at the beginning of the discussion as a means of starting discussion on grounds that paticipants will perceive as safe.

Sometimes the decision about when to present your own views will be made for you, for someone will ask, "Well, Betty, you've been researching critical thinking for a long time. You haven't said anything about it yet. What do you think it is?" But whether you're cast in the role of participant by someone else or by your own choice, you must always *maintain the same objective stance towards yourself as you would towards others.* That allows you to be completely frank in expressing your opinions, yet allows you to avoid defensiveness. For example, you might reply, "I find myself in strong disagreement with George's idea that critical thinking is primarily computational skill. It *is* that, of course, but much more; for instance . . ." Having then spelled out your position, you might then ask George what he thinks in reply, thereby passing the ball—your ball—back to the group.

If possible, let others then take up the defense or the reply to the reply and revert to your role as referee. This is not an easy maneuver, but the following cautions and practices will help you to address key issues in your double capacity, with minimal risk to your face and status as discussion leader. Indeed, they apply to anyone addressing key issues, but especially apply to the leader whose job it is to preserve his or her own face *and everyone else's* face.*

- *Discipline yourself not to regard winning as getting your way* but as joining others in doing the best possible job of thinking things through. This is difficult to do when your own opinions are at stake, but also at stake is your leadership role, a role you must play well for the benefit of all.

- *Present your views forcefully but tentatively* (never judgmentally) as one among other opinions to be considered. For example, you may want to preface your remarks by saying, "Another slant to consider here is . . ." or "Has anyone given any thought to the idea that . . ." thereby putting some distance between you and your opinions.

- *Protect yourself against your own unspoken assumptions* by saying, "Unless I've overlooked something, it seems to me . . ." or "Did I miss something?" Since so much of your work as leader is eliciting other people's assumptions, you don't want to be caught out making foolish ones of your own. But if you are caught out, simply treat a challenge to your views as one more thing for the group to consider. For ex-

*"Normally everybody's face depends on everybody else's being maintained" (Brown and Levinson 1987, p. 61).

ample, George challenges you by saying: "Aren't you in danger of stretching the notion of thinking all out of proportion, Betty?" You reply as leader, "In what way, George?" After George has responded, you elicit comments from the group.

- *Encourage people to express differing views* that will help everyone to arrive at the best interpretation or make the best decision, inviting them to consider your evidence, arguments, and interests, and offering to consider theirs. "I really would appreciate your comments," or "No doubt some of you disagree. Could we hear from you now?"

- *By your own example, urge people to make creative use of conflicting opinions.* Weigh the merits of differing views carefully and accept criticism gracefully. This doesn't mean giving in at the first sign of resistance to your views, but it does mean maintaining a dispassionate attitude towards them. If participants see you getting hot under the collar, that heat will spread like wildfire.

- *Never respond in kind to hostile or angry accusations by others,* for then you lose composure and all claim to rationality and evenhandedness. Imagine someone says to you,"Betty, that's idiotic! You'd have to be really dumb to think that." You reply: "Could we hear your reasons to the contrary of the view I've expressed?" By *ignoring the insult and stressing the merits or demerits of the case,* you avoid escalation of hostility, save your face and the accuser's face, and keep the talk on a rational plane—just the opposite of what would ensue if you were to reply, "Who are you to call *me* dumb, when everything you've said up to now is crap!"

OPPOSING AND SUPPORTING OTHERS

Both as discussion leader and as participant, you will want to support or to oppose one or another of the views expressed. That is in the nature of pro-and-con reasoning and inquiry generally. Here, we're concerned with the social aspect of the everyday reasoning process, that is, with the social dynamic that allows you to disagree with an opinion without alienating those who support it and agree with an opinion without alienating those who oppose it.

Opposing Others

Opposing others means opposing their views but supporting them as people. In genuine inquiry, you want people to disagree with you. They may be right, or they might have a better idea or may help you to work out a better one. Here are some of the things you can do to gain maximum benefit from disagreement:

- *Find fault with ideas, not with the persons who present them;* for example, question the worth of the plan, not the competence of the planner. "How could you come up with such a ridiculous notion?" is a surefire provocation, from which nothing profitable is likely to result.

- *Acknowledge the merits of a person's position* before you criticize it or present evidence or arguments supporting a different or opposing position. Something like, "I readily see the advantages of George's view, for example [list one or two]; however, I'd like to suggest another line on this topic."

- *Whenever you can, instead of attacking bad ideas, introduce good ones without saying they are better,* in order to save the opposition's face. For example, "Maybe there's another interpretation to consider here . . ." or "What about the possibility that . . ."

- *Again, to save face, let people finish talking when you think they are wrong* rather than interrupting to correct them or otherwise making evident your displeasure or impatience.

- *Encourage people to disagree with you freely* by responding objectively, not defensively, when they say you are wrong. As mentioned before, such openness saves face and makes progress.

- *When things aren't going your way, get smart,* don't get mad. Request a review of participants' thinking thus far, giving you time to recoup, to suggest revisions, to raise questions, to challenge meanings and evidence.

Supporting Others

Supporting others means supporting them as people and contributing to their self-esteem, not just supporting their ideas. Agreement is face-enhancing in itself, but you also need to encourage the further participation of the person you're agreeing with. Here are some things you can do to amplify the benefits of agreement and support:

- *Look for good ideas in the thinking of others,* not only in their formal arguments, but in their humor, asides, and novel suggestions, in their idle musings, and in the way they bring their experiences to bear on the issue. For example, "I was especially interested, Paul, in how your teaching experience helped to clarify your view of critical thinking."

- *Show appreciation for good ideas* by saying how they will work to everyone's benefit, by showing how to make them work, and by spelling out their advantages over other rival claims.

- *Introduce a better idea as a friendly amendment,* requesting comment. For example, "What would you say to a somewhat different approach . . . ?" or "Would you be willing to consider this qualification [addition, rider, condition] . . . ?"

- *Credit others for contributing to your thinking,* saying, for instance, "You've mentioned something I wasn't aware of, which gives me an idea . . ." This is a particularly face-enhancing courtesy.

- *Acknowledge others' tact, frankness, patience, good humor,* quick-wittedness and imagination by words, gestures and expressions of approval.

- *Don't get smug when things are going your way;* instead, be solicitous: ask others how ideas, events, proposals, decisions as they now stand will affect their interests, their own thinking, and so forth.

CONCLUDING A DISCUSSION

As you well know, many discussions are either too short or too long and are ineffectual or inconclusive, overwrought or underdone. Informal discussions perhaps suffer least from these afflictions either because they are easier to conduct or to break off, or because there is frequently less at stake than in formal discussions of the sort we have been describing.

Formal discussions suffer for two reasons: either too much is jammed into too short a time or too much time is allotted for too little. The latter is the more destructive situation, leading inevitably to boredom and digression. As any entertainer will tell you, "Leave 'em wanting more." By contrast, the problem of allowing too little time is more readily rectified by scheduling another session. Deferral is better than being bored alive.

The obvious solution to both problems is a well-planned agenda with definite, realistic time limits. That way, the awkwardnesses of trailing off into irrelevancies or of being cut off in mid-sentence are avoided. So, knowing when to quit is partly, at least, a matter of simply judging how long it will take to do the job.

A rough guideline is this: the more technical and objective the issue, the more predictable the time requirements for discussion. The more controversial and contentious the issue, the less predictable the time requirements. Time can also be a problem in those situations earlier described in which people require to be "brought up to speed" during the course of the discussion.

Only rarely is it advisable to allow for indefinite time, to let discussion go on for as long as it takes to reach some desired result or until things just peter out. One of the authors recalls a seminar in graduate school during which five giants in the fields of philosophy, psychology, and linguistics convened a discussion of symbolism in cognition that went on for ten hours! With only about twenty people in the room at a time, all vitally interested, it was a riveting experience. But that is a rare and magical occurrence.

Reconcilable Differences: Consensus

To keep a discussion going beyond when an acceptable consensus has been reached is to invite trouble. A perverse tendency to faultfinding for its own sake and wrangling over minor details are the most likely result followed closely by blind charges down corridors of irrelevancy. Before that happens, ask people if their *primary* concerns have been met; also ask if there is anything further *directly relevant to the topic under discussion* to be considered; and if not, cut the meeting off then and there with a polite, "Thank you all for your contribution." If there is to be a follow-up meeting or further discussion of related topics, now is the time to announce it (at least the date and time of the meeting) with a full agenda to follow.

Differences You Don't Have to Reconcile: Agreeing to Disagree

In many cases, *agreement is not a necessary conclusion to a discussion.* Unlike negotiation, which aims at getting to "yes," a discussion, in the fundamental sense of *inquiry,* may be considered a rousing success if it gets to "maybe," and often falls far short of that. Because inquiry concerns discovery and the quest for new knowledge and insight, the discussions involved can continue for weeks, years, or generations. Science and most forms of research involve discussion verbally and in print that goes on indefinitely. Any *particular* discussion, therefore, need not be conclusive. Indeed, it may not be in the best interests of inquiry or truth that it be so.

Because of the difficulty that some people have living with perpetual doubt, the inconclusiveness of many discussions, particularly those of an academic or theoretical nature, is disturbing to them. But the price of premature closure on an issue of continuing significance, such as the causes of cancer, the control of international terrorism, environmental pollution, and the like, could be very high: namely, false security and ignorance. For that reason alone it is important to agree to disagree until conclusive evidence or arguments one way or the other emerge.

Where a pressing decision has to be made, where discussion is a matter of practical reasoning toward that decision, permanent suspension of judgment will of course not do. But in areas where people conduct inquiry and discovery for their own sake, it is the *only* thing that will do. Inquiry in those areas never ends, and neither do the discussions that mediate it. Still, physically, psychologically and socially we have to know when to quit for the time being. Even the ten-hour discussion of symbolism and cognition mentioned above came to a halt when everybody decided that dinner was way overdue!

Generally speaking, a simple time limit set in advance, as with a seminar or regularly scheduled discussion group, will do the trick. Most research seminars in science and scholarship are like that. People meet to advance their latest ideas and test them against conflicting opinion and argumentation, hoping that something new will surface. Frequently something new does turn up; just as frequently, it doesn't. But that is no reason to be discouraged, for tomorrow is another day, and with it comes another chance, and yet another and another, to continue the dialogue. That continuing dialogue increases rapport among participants and makes fine-grained distinctions and contributions possible. As Descartes reminded us in his *Meditations,* systematic doubt is one of our most powerful weapons in the war against ignorance and in the quest for knowledge. By it, good ideas survive to serve us better and bad ones are ditched, their failures serving to instruct us.

Instead of looking for closure or consensus in open-ended discussions, look for a natural breaking-off point, a phase in the continuing dialogue where it is convenient to stop and from which it will be possible to pick up next time. There are no rules for making that judgment, but keeping track of the discussion is the best preparation for making it. And that brings us to the question of how to take notes, addressed in Chapter 10, which follows.

CHAPTER 10

On Taking Notes: From Thinking Aloud to Thinking on Paper

WHY TAKE NOTES?

Taking notes helps you to conduct a discussion by compensating for the limitations of your short-term memory and allowing you to focus on the spontaneous *thinking* that is going on.

While listening to others, you may jot down the questions they ask, the answers they give or get, their major points, key facts, or lines of argument taken. You can also note questions to ask, points to make, evidence to cite, or arguments to pursue.

The key to taking notes effectively is identifying what is important to record, what isn't, and why. For that, you need a *listening plan*. Without a listening plan, you may miss crucial points, waste energy worrying that you will miss them, or cost yourself opportunities for participation by trying to write everything down for fear of missing something really important. Without a listening plan, you may also be prone to incomplete or incoherent note taking. Later review of such notes may leave you asking, "What on earth did I [or they] mean by that?" "What is the relevance of this item?" "How does all this junk hang together?" "What really went on at that meeting?" If your present habits of note taking leave you in a chronic state of wondering what was said, by whom, and why, then this chapter is for you.

ON BECOMING A GOOD LISTENER

Answers to the questions What's important?, What isn't?, and Why? will vary somewhat with your perspective as leader, participant, or recorder of a discussion. In other words, how you take notes will depend mostly on why you want to take them: to enable you to *lead* a discussion more effectively, to *participate* more effectively, or to *write* more effectively at a later time, converting thinking aloud to thinking on paper.

Suppose you want to participate more effectively. Then you can plan to track whatever thinking develops as discussion proceeds, noting key points of interest to you, without imposing any special organization. If, on the other hand, you want to lead a discussion more effectively, then, keeping your agenda in mind, you will want to focus on who says what about what or decides what about what. Taking notes for purposes of *writing about the topic* later on represents an *extension of the process of inquiry* itself, a continuation of the discussion on paper.

As leader, you can take notes privately, keeping your words to yourself until you need to use them. Or you can take notes publicly on a chalkboard or flipchart, where everybody can see what you write when you write it. Either way, you free others from the need to take extensive notes themselves while supplying them with the basis of agreement (or disagreement) on what was said or decided. You also supply yourself with a basis for putting appropriate questions to the right people and for summarizing the proceedings. In short, by taking notes you gain leverage for directing discussion and ensuring that it will be productive.

Whether you take notes privately or publicly depends on how *visibly* you want to lead. You avoid drawing attention to yourself when you take them privately—an advantage if you want to play the collegial or facilitative roles described in Chapter Three. In addition, you avoid giving your notes the authority of writing, because you do not introduce them into discussion as *written* discourse. Rather, you use them to help yourself to contribute *orally* to *spoken* discourse.

Taking your notes publicly enables you to conduct a discussion not only by speaking and listening, but also by writing and moving about—an advantage if you want to play the directive or instructional roles described in Chapter Three. When you get up to write, you draw attention to yourself and focus attention on your words. While you are writing on a chalkboard or flipchart, you can comment on the progress of discussion and edit it for content without really interrupting it. "Correct me if I'm wrong, but the following claims seem to have emerged thus far" is a convenient phrase to use on such occasions. You thereby encourage people to participate by giving them visible recognition for their ideas; and when you again take your seat among them, you refocus their attention on each other through the statements you have recorded.

ON BECOMING "FLIPPANT"

Flipcharts combine the visibility of the chalkboard with the flexibility of the notebook. Unlined and measuring 27 by 34 inches, they come in pads of twenty sheets and are usually mounted on a tripod easel for easy display. (In manufacturers' catalogs, flipcharts are often called "easel pads.") Individual sheets can be separated from the pad along perforations at the top (for posting side by side) or flipped back over the top, notebook fashion—hence the commonly used name.

Flipcharts have particular advantages. For example, you don't have to erase anything to make room for something else; therefore, you can preserve your data for later display or retrieval as needed. Individual sheets can be posted around the room while the meeting is in progress, and also can be taken away for future reference.

The versatility of flipcharts makes them especially useful for guiding discussion of complex subjects. Accordingly, we will illustrate their use in generating what elsewhere we call a "topical draft," a basic articulation and organization of ideas, facts, and arguments for purposes of producing a written document (Howard and Barton 1986, pages 32–36).

To produce a topical draft of a discussion, you organize the results of discussion *as they emerge* by putting topical *labels* on statements, claims, facts, and arguments. To label properly, you think *bifocally,* focusing not only on *what* is said but also on *where* it belongs in the larger scheme of things. You may find that kind of thinking a little awkward at first, but with practice you will soon acquire the habit of asking yourself, "Now what is the main point here and where does it belong?"

The listening and note-taking plan we present below is designed for the leader-participant whose difficult job it is to direct and contribute to a discussion while recording the proceedings. Frequently, a discussion leader is expected to draft a document reflecting the main points, arguments, facts and evidence cited, and conclusions, if any, reached. The following suggestions will help you to do that with a minimum of effort and a maximum of efficiency.

FROM TALK TO TOPICAL DRAFT

Suppose you are asked to conduct a detailed situation analysis (see Chapter Five) to be followed by a write-up of the same. Here's how we suggest you might proceed.

To keep participants oriented, you may want to post a flipchart version of your agenda at the front of the room. If not, be sure that everyone has a copy of the agenda at hand. That agenda, incidentally, is also your tentative outline for the write-up to come later. Draw attention to the agenda as you start your introduction, proposing a schedule for discussion of each topic so participants will understand what is at issue and can ask you questions and suggest changes. Such preliminaries are useful particularly if you are pressed for time and results. If time is not short, if this is but one of a series of continuing discussions, be content with "maybe's" and don't force a schedule on the proceedings. If, on the other hand, the group is under pressure for results, conclude your introductory remarks by setting a schedule specifying when you plan to begin and end the major parts of the meeting.

During the meeting, leave your flipchart agenda posted so participants can follow the progress of the discussion. Here's how your agenda might look after you've decided on the topics, their sequence, and a schedule:

SITUATION ANALYSIS

08:30–08:45 Introduction

08:45–10:15 Part 1: What is going on?
      1.1 Threats and opportunities
      1.2 Our strengths and weaknesses

10:15–10:30 Break

10:30–12:00 <u>Part 2</u>:   What do we do?

                    2.1 What are the options?
                    2.2 How do they compare?
                    2.3 Which do we prefer?

12:00   <u>Lunch</u>

You have a choice in your use of flipcharts. Using *one* set of flipcharts, you can take up Parts 1 and 2 in sequence, creating separate sets of notes and separate summary sheets for each of the subtopics, the latter to be posted where participants can easily see them. Or you can use *two* sets of flipcharts to create two sets of notes corresponding to Parts 1 and 2. As a general rule, the more complex the issues, the better it is to use separate sets of flipcharts for the major divisions of the discussion. By keeping matters sorted in this manner you can eliminate much confusion and allow people ready access to ground already covered. For example, you can always say, "Well, George, you recall this point? [*Flip to it*] Now, do you still hold to it, or do you want to qualify it?"

Discussing complex issues requires people to address interrelated topics and questions like those numbered 1.1 to 2.3 in the example above. As a result, people are very likely to say something important about one topic or question while addressing another. In addition, live thinking is seldom linear, despite the fact that in writing its results will eventually be presented in linear fashion. Live thinking doubles back, crisscrosses itself, finds exceptions and new directions spontaneously. For that reason, we recommend that you create a *filing system* using topical labels and a numbering system like the one illustrated above, based on the major parts and subdivisions of the agenda. Use the numbering system to identify what major topic or subtopic the speaker was addressing when you noted down a particular statement. Use a topical label to describe the nature of the statement.

The topical label is a word, a phrase, a name, anything that says how to *classify* a statement or proposal or idea. "Exceptions to the rule," "possible effects," "new problems," "additional opportunities," "possible options if . . . ," "unforeseen difficulties," "safe recommendations," "risky recommendations," and so on. Such notations are like marginalia to the running text of the discussion whose broad course is guided by the agenda. You enter your notations here and there as need indicates. Then, for example, if "unforeseen difficulties" begin to receive major emphasis, you can make a separate sheet for them, listing them as they emerge and noting where they come up, say, under 1.1 or 2.2.

Use labels to identify the nature of subjects that come up over and over as you move through the agenda. Use the same label to clarify them each time they come up. That way, you generate a network of ideas that is like the map of a difficult landscape. And that is exactly what you are after: a conceptual plot of the progress of inquiry. Such labels establish *connections*. And connections are vital to your writing efforts later on, helping you to *compose* the results of discussion.

KEEPING CATEGORIES IN MIND

Many statements and claims concern categories of discourse that you may want to label in your notes. Many disputes concern *definitions*—statements of what something is and what it isn't. Others concern what *differences* or *comparisons* really matter; and yet others have to do with *explanations* and *facts* (including various sorts of data).

For example, *Is abortion a form of murder?* That question will start a dispute about definitions. *Can one equate the circumstances of a small rural community with those of a drug-ridden urban setting in considering the issues of abortion?* That is a question of valid comparison. *What is the incidence of teenage pregnancy in community X? Why does it occur so frequently (or infrequently) in that community?* Those are questions looking for facts and explanations.

Questions of meaning, of comparison, of fact and explanation receive logically different sorts of answers. But the anwers may *look* the same in your notes if you don't identify what type of question was being addressed. For example, a statement offered as *a fact* and subject to challenge as a fact could appear to be a statement offered *in explanation* of something, and hence subject to very different types of challenge. So, as a general strategy, ask yourself the following as discussion goes on:

- Is this a matter of *definition,* of what a word means, of the kind of thing it is, of what it includes or excludes, or what it does, or how it works?

- Is this a matter of *comparison,* of how one thing differs from another, how it is similar or different in degree or kind?

- Is this a matter of *explanation,* of what causes something, or what effects it has, what weighs in for or against it in the way of evidence or factual information?

Ask yourself, and others, "Are you offering us a definition? Are there exceptions to your definition?" "What are the significant contrasts or differences you have in mind?" "What is your evidence, what solid facts can you cite to support your position?" These questions, more than any others, can help you to keep matters focused and on the plane of objectivity. Insist on them, if necessary, pressing people to back up their claims and engaging others to probe the issues along lines of definition, significant contrast, and evidence. Meanwhile, note down their responses on a flipchart, using topical labels wherever needed.

After the discussion has ended, you can transfer your notes to topically labeled index cards to gather and organize information. You can also use your computer, employing programs like *Squarenote 3.0* (Union Squareware 1989). *Squarenote 3.0* allows you to record notes at great length, collect and organize your notes, arrange them under different headings, and print all or a selection of them, and it gives you access to any bit of information under any heading.

THE FUNCTION OF WRITING FORMATS IN DISCUSSION

We use the term *formats* to refer to standard writing structures, such as the essay, the office memo, the business report, or the proposal. If, in advance of a formal discussion, you know that you will be expected to produce a document in one of the standard formats, use that format both to structure your agenda and as a supply of convenient topical labels. For example, if a business proposal is your eventual writing task, your headings and labels may include all or a selection of the following: Introduction and Background; Situation Analysis; Approach, Objectives, and Action Plan; Relevant Experience, Organizational Capability, and Project Staffing; Schedule, Costs, and Closing.

The function of formats is to provide a framework for thinking in writing (Howard and Barton 1986, page 42).

Far from being straitjackets into which the products of thought have to be uncomfortably fitted, formats from the standard essay to the legal brief to the scientific report are instruments of thinking and discovery as well as aids to the composition of ideas. That composition begins, however, during discussion; and therein lies the additional function of formats, namely, to give tentative shape to a discussion. We say "tentative" shape because, as mentioned, a discussion may meander in ways that the written presentation of its results does not. Also, the order of live inquiry, exploration and discovery, not to mention dialogue, is not the same as, or only partially overlaps with, the strictly logical order of argument. Nevertheless, as abstract forms, formats can be valuable guides to the ordering and labeling of ideas as they emerge from discussion.

This is not a book on writing as such, but obviously, formal and informal discussion are often preliminary steps to writing. What we have tried to do here is to outline a practical strategy and simple procedures for linking the two, for taking that first step from talking to writing. The use of topical labels drawn from your agenda or eventual format, or spontaneously generated on the spot, represents an early phase of composition. In effect, *the collection of flipcharts with their messy scrawls, diagrams, numbers, and labels constitutes a first draft of your document ripe for further revision.* If you would like further guidance in the writing process, particularly the later phases of composition and expression, you may want to consult Chapter Two, "From First to Last Draft: Generating, Composing, and Expressing Ideas," of our book *Thinking on Paper* (1986). As well, many useful guides to technical, business, scientific, and academic writing exist from which you may select the formats appropriate to your subject or discipline.

Appendix A: Suggested Viewing

A critical, comparative study of selected television shows may help you gain skill as a leader of rational discussion, remembering, of course, that your purpose is never to entertain an audience.

If you want to make such a study, we recommend that you first review Chapter Three of this book, "Choosing a Leadership Role," Chapter Four, "Preparing a Discussion Plan," and Chapter Nine, "Behaving Thoughtfully: The Do's and Don'ts." Then compare what you see on television with what you believe are appropriate ways for *you* to lead discussion.

Here's a representative selection of regularly scheduled television shows differing in format and style of leadership.

For examples of the roundtable format, we suggest *Washington Week in Review* and *Wall Street Week*. Both are peer-discussion programs led by a moderator who also participates as an equal. Other examples include *Meet the Press, Face the Nation,* and the *McLaughlin Group.* The latter, as contrasted with a slower-paced program such as *Wall Street Week,* exemplifies a driven, rushed, bluntly confrontational format.

The many so-called talk shows on television fall into three basic categories: the one-on-one sustained discussion (e.g., *A Conversation with Bill Moyers* on PBS, William F. Buckley's *Firing Line,* and in Canada, Brian Lennehan's *City Lights*); the successive-interview format (e.g., the *Tonight Show* with a succession of hosts, not to mention many other late-night clones of that well-established format); and the one-on-many audience-and-panel format (e.g., the type pioneered by Phil Donahue and lately copied by many others).

The successive-interview format is also used extensively by many newscasts but with primary focus on noteworthy events and issues rather than "personalities" or celebrities. ABC's *Nightline* and PBS's *MacNeil/Lehrer NewsHour* are examples of pointed discussions of world events where interviewees, usually of opposing viewpoints, are put on the spot by the moderator. In Canada, CBC's *Journal* is the equivalent. Ask yourself why you might prefer one newscast over another.

Appendix B: The Parliamentary Method

When using the Method of Personification to over-come discussion stage-fright, as explained in Chapter Two, you may find your characters appear entirely negative or recalcitrant to direct persuasion. Then you may want to try a variation on the Method of Personification. We call this variation the Parliamentary Method. It consists of positing a third party—a jury, judge, or parliamentary chairperson—who really is open to your ideas. In other words, you don't try to persuade the negative voice but rather talk *past* that voice to a third party who can be convinced. "Madam Chair, I realize that my learned friend is utterly convinced that I am a phony and a fraud, but I urge you to consider whether I would be undertaking this risky task of speaking up on an issue of importance to the company if that were so? I ask for dismissal of these charges and of the persons who made them so I can get on with my business." Or some such conceit.

The basic strategy here is that you *appear* to be addressing your inner adversary but actually are addressing a neutral party who is listening to *you* very carefully and considering the merits of your case at face value—no lingering history or past judgments attached. You speak directly to the neutral body, and indirectly to your adversary, as if a lot of rational people were listening. The latter at least *can* be convinced and enable you, first, to put distance between yourself and your negative inner voices while making your case; second, to absolve yourself of their charges; and third, have the third party banish your accusers from the scene—rather like a legal restraining order for the duration of your business.

Bibliography

Argyris, Christopher. *Reasoning, Learning and Action: Individual and Organizational.* San Francisco: Jossey-Bass, 1982.

Beck, Aaron T. *Cognitive Therapy and Emotional Disorders.* New York: American Library, 1979.

Brown, Penelope and Stephen C. Levinson. *Politeness: Some Universals in Language Usage.* New York: Cambridge University Press, 1987.

Burns, David D. *Feeling Good: The New Mood Therapy.* New York: William Morrow, 1980.

Deep, Sam and Lyle Sussman. *Smart Moves.* New York: Addison-Wesley, 1990.

Descartes, René. *Meditations,* in *The Philosophical Works of Descartes,* Vol. II. Translated by Elizabeth S. Haldane and G.R.T. Ross. Cambridge, England: Cambridge University Press, 1955.

Fisher, Roger F. and William Ury. *Getting to Yes: Negotiating Agreement Without Giving In.* New York: Penguin Books, 1983.

Fisher, Roger F. and Scott Brown. *Getting Together: Building a Relationship That Gets to Yes.* New York: Viking Penguin, 1989.

The Forum Corporation. *Influence Management.* The Forum, One Exchange Place, Boston, Massachusetts 02109. Seminar materials are copyright 1982. Reference is to ideas presented in the seminar, not to a publication.

Frank, Milo O. *How to Run a Successful Meeting in Half the Time.* New York: Pocket Books, 1989.

Grice, Paul. *Studies in the Way of Words.* Cambridge, Mass.: Harvard University Press, 1989.

Howard, V. A. and J. H. Barton. *Thinking on Paper.* New York: William Morrow, 1986.

Howard, V. A. *Varieties of Thinking.* New York: Routledge, Chapman & Hall, 1990.

Kinneavy, James F. *A Theory of Discourse.* New York: W. W. Norton & Co., 1980.

Lewis, C. S. *The Screwtape Letters.* New York: Macmillan, 1962.

Lockwood, Alan H. "Medical Problems of Musicians," in *The New England Journal of Medicine,* 26 January 1989, pp. 221–248.

Mager, Robert F. *Preparing Instructional Objectives,* revised 2nd ed. Belmont, Ca.: Lake Publishing Company, 1984. Earlier editions copyright 1962, 1975.

———. *Goal Analysis,* 2nd ed. Belmont, Ca.: Lake Publishing Company, 1984. First edition copyright 1972.

———. and Peter Pipe. *Analyzing Performance Problems or Your Really Oughta Wanna.* Belmont, Ca.: Fearon Publishers, 1970. Second Edition, 1984, Belmont, Ca.: Lake Publishing Co.

Perkins, David N. *The Mind's Best Work.* Cambridge, Mass.: Harvard University Press, 1981.

Perkins, David N., R. Allen, and J. Hafner. "Difficulties in Everyday Reasoning," in *Thinking: The Expanding Frontier.* William Maxwell, ed. Hillsdale, N.J.: Lawrence Erlbaum Assocs., 1983.

Perkins, David N., and Edward E. Smith. *The Teaching of Thinking.* Hillsdale, N.J.: Lawrence Erlbaum Assocs., 1985.

Plato. "Republic" and "Apology," in *The Collected Dia-*

logues. Edith Hamilton and Huntington Cairns, eds. New York: Random House, 1963.

Ristad, Eloise. *A Soprano on Her Head.* Moab, Utah: Real People Press, 1982.

Robert, H. M. *Robert's Rules of Order.* New York: Bell, 1978.

Scheffler, Israel. *Conditions of Knowledge.* Chicago: Scott, Foresman, 1965.

Squarenote 3.0. Brookline, MA. Union Squareware, 1989. Available from the company at 27 St. Mary's Court, Brookline, MA 02140. Price: $99.00.

Index

About the Authors

Vernon A. Howard, Ph.D., is co-founder and co-director with Israel Scheffler of the Philosophy of Education Research Center at Harvard University. He is the author of five other books and numerous articles on aspects of symbolism and critical thinking. He also consults to businesses, colleges, and universities on writing and discussion skills. Howard has taught at universities in Canada, England, and the United States and is the recipient of several major fellowships, among them three Exxon Education Foundation grants, two Latsis Foundation grants (with Israel Scheffler), and a John Dewey Senior Fellowship. He lives in Cambridge, Massachusetts.

James H. Barton, M.A., has thirty years' experience as a writer and management educator, beginning his career as a reporter for the *New York Journal of Commerce* and staff writer for *Forbes Magazine*. Subsequently, Barton served as senior consultant and project manager for leading management consulting firms specializing in human resource development. They include Sterling Institute, Inc., and the Forum Corporation of North America, where he designed and developed management education materials and seminars for key government agencies and major U.S. corporations. He is now an author, editorial consultant, and Associate of the Philosophy of Education Research Center. He lives with his family in Cambridge, Massachusetts.